BANNOCKBURN
1314

BANNOCKBURN
1314

CHRIS BROWN

First published 2013 by
Spellmount, an imprint of
The History Press
The Mill, Brimscombe Port
Stroud, Gloucestershire, GL5 2QG
www.thehistorypress.co.uk

British Library Cataloguing in Publication Data.
A catalogue record for this book is available from the British Library.

ISBN 978 0 7524 9759 4

Typesetting and origination by The History Press
Printed in Great Britain

CONTENTS

Acknowledgements	7
List of Illustrations	8
Introduction	13
Timeline	19
Historical Background	21
The Armies	46
The Commanders	46
The Soldiers	57
The Tactics	75
Before the Battle	84
Edward II's Forces	84
Robert I's Forces	90
The Battlefield	98
After the Battle	132
The Legacy	144
Orders of Battle	149
Further Reading	151
Index	152

ACKNOWLEDGEMENTS

As ever, I am primarily indebted to my wife, Pat, who has borne the brunt of moaning, whingeing and frustration that is part and parcel of me writing a book, and to my editor at The History press, Jo De Vries, whose patience seemingly knows no bounds. I am also indebted to the various societies who have, from time to time, invited me to give presentations about this remarkable battle. I like to think that the many questions that I have been asked at such events have helped to make me more aware of the wide range of factors that forged the environment and influenced the processes that made things turn out the way they did. Finally, I am indebted to three kings: Edward I, Edward II and Robert I, as well as, of course, the people of fourteenth-century England and Scotland, without whom – as they say – none of this would have been possible.

LIST OF ILLUSTRATIONS

1. Inchcolm Abbey, where – over 100 years after the event – Abbott Bower penned a highly colourful description of the battle.
2. A page from Sir Thomas Grey's *Scalacronica*.
3. The coronation of Edward I. Edward only commanded one Scottish action in person, the Battle of Falkirk, 1298. His death in 1307 was a major blow to the fortunes of the English occupation forces, however the tide of the war had probably already started to turn in favour of the Scots.
4. A sixteenth-century English artwork, depicting a fictitious parliament of Edward I attended by Llewellyn, Prince of Wales and Alexander III. Artworks and forged documents were an important weapon in the propaganda arsenals of medieval kings: the 'Dodgy Dossier' is not a modern innovation.
5. John Balliol, from a Scottish amorial illuminated between 1581 and 1584. The king is surrounded by the broken symbols of his rule.
6. Illuminated capital from an English medieval document depicting a scene from the siege of Carlisle.

7. The obverse and reverse of the seal of Edward I.
8. Significant towns and castles in late medieval Scotland.
9. A silver penny of Robert I. Pennies of a given weight and purity of silver were known as 'sterlings' (a term that originated from Germany) and were acceptable right across Europe.
10. The Great Seal of Robert I.
11. The memorial of Angus Og, Lord of the Isles. Although he was a vital supporter of Robert I's kingship from 1307 onward, it is not clear whether he was present at Bannockburn.
12. Detail from a Scottish grave effigy showing a fourteenth-century soldier with bascinet, padded jack and the 'heater'-shaped shield typical of the period.
13. An assemblage of plate armour to protect the arm. Pieces as sophisticated as this one were still relatively rare in 1314 and would have been very much the province of the wealthy or of men who spent a large proportion of their time in military service.
14/15. A mail hauberk might be worn underneath a padded garment or on top of it. Opinion was divided about the relative effectiveness.
16. A re-enactor wearing the sort of brase and hose generally worn under clothing.
17. Closed helmets of this style were definitely old-fashioned by 1314, but were still serviceable and likely to have been passed on to the rank and file from better-equipped men-at-arms.
18. A selection of ordinary personal effects: a dagger, flint and steel, leather pouch, rosary and dice.
19. A man-at-arms and a spearman. The man-at-arms is wearing particularly extensive and heavy mail. By 1314 pieces of plate armour – particularly at the shoulder and elbow – were being added to supplement mail.

20. A *chapel-de-fer* or 'iron hat'. These were widely used throughout northern and western Europe in the thirteenth and fourteenth centuries.

21. It was possible, though a little difficult, to don mail unaided. Note the thickness of the padded garment under the mail.

22. A party of medieval spearmen would have looked rather like this, though the spears would have been a good deal longer.

23. A close-up of the same party of spearmen. Although individuals were responsible for the acquisition of their own equipment, there were well-understood minimum standards which had to be observed.

24. An archer bending his bow. Although a skilled archer could hit a man at 300 yards, the arrow was unlikely to inflict serious damage on even a lightly armoured man.

25. A typical fourteenth-century archer.

26. Very few soldiers would have had the luxury of a sophisticated tent like this one.

27. With their spear points presented to the enemy in a thick hedge, a schiltrom was virtually invulnerable to cavalry attacks.

28. Articulated armour for the legs and arms was becoming increasingly common by 1314. This re-enactor is mounted on a 'covered' or 'barded' horse, though in the fourteenth century the barding would have consisted of several layers of cloth to reduce the effectiveness of arrows and edged weapons.

29. Grave effigy of Sir Roger de Trumpington. This image dates from about 1280; by the time of Bannockburn the absence of any plate armour other than knee protection would have made the bearer look rather outdated, but would still have been acceptable as equipment for a man-at-arms

30. Looking south from the approximate position of King Robert's division on the afternoon of 23 June.

31. The contemporary material indicates that the Scots moved down to the plain from higher ground in the New Park. They probably formed up in the area where the new Bannockburn High School stands.

32. Once the Scots had formed up they had to negotiate this steep slope before deploying on the plain.

33. A Scottish 'birlinn' or galley. Vessels like this were used extensively by Robert I in his campaigns on the west coast of Scotland. A number of barons and other landholders were obliged to provide manned warships like this for their 'knight service' rather than serving as mounted men-at-arms, though it was not uncommon for such men to serve in both capacities as required.

34. The Battle of Bannockburn as envisaged by Oman and Gardiner, though it bears very little resemblance to the contemporary source material.

35. The open farmland on which the main battle took place. Contrary to Victorian interpretations, all of the contemporary material makes it clear that the main engagement took place on firm ground, not among bogs and marshes.

36. The Bannock burn. The burn was probably rather wider in 1314, but even today it has a very soft and muddy floor which would be a considerable barrier to armoured men trying to escape the battlefield.

37. A view toward 'The Entry', where the Earls of Gloucester and Hereford made the first attack and where de Bohun was killed in a single combat with King Robert.

38. A well-equipped infantry man of the fourteenth century, with a *chapel-de-fer* helmet and two thin, padded garments, one under his mail and another over it.

39. The sole remaining building of Cambuskenneth Abbey. During the night of 23/24 June, the Earl of Athol mounted an attack on King Robert's stores. Of the four actions of the battle, this is the only one of which the precise location can be identified without question.
40. A well-intentioned re-enactor in the tradition of *Brigadoon* meets *Braveheart*; however, neither kilts nor two-handed swords have any relevance to the fourteenth century.
41. The head of a battle-hammer allegedly recovered from Bannockburn battlefield.
42. Letter patent of John Balliol, acknowledging the feudal superiority of Edward I.
43. The seal of John Balliol.
44. The Pilkington Jackson statue of Robert I at the National Trust for Scotland's Bannockburn Visitor Centre.
45. The nineteenth-century brass effigy of King Robert from his burial place at Dunfermline Abbey; in the 1330s the tombs of both King Robert and his queen – Elizabeth de Burgh – were destroyed by English troops.

INTRODUCTION

The Battle of Bannockburn has become the subject of a considerable range of romantic – and in some cases rather unromantic – mythologising. Quite why this should be the case is a bit of a mystery in itself; there is really very little of any importance that we do not know about this battle. The contemporary and near-contemporary source material is actually quite extensive and contains sufficient data to provide us with a reasonably coherent picture of the nature of the armies and of the course of the Battle of Bannockburn. As we would expect, the value of the record material is really limited to information about the political situation and some insight concerning enlistment, supplies and the progress to the battlefield; it offers us very little indeed about the battle itself beyond a basic outline of the progress of the engagements.

Overall there is surprisingly little contradiction between the different chronicle writers, though all of them must be used with caution: each of the authors had an agenda and not all narrative material is of equal value. Walter Bower's *Scotichronicon* was not written until more than a century after Bannockburn; it is wildly inaccurate and virulently anti-English. On the other hand, Sir Thomas Grey, author of *Scalacronica*,

1. Inchcolm Abbey, where – over 100 years after the event – Abbott Bower penned a highly colourful description of the battle.

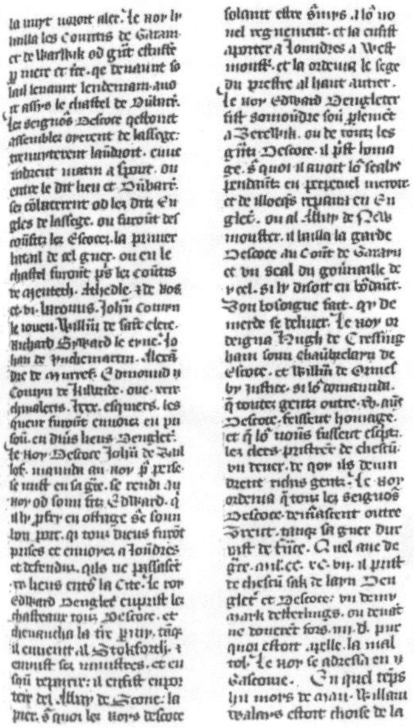

2. A page from Sir Thomas Grey's Scalacronica.

NARRATIVE EVIDENCE

This is the collective term for all chronicle material. The monastic chronicle from Lanercost has a brief but useful account of the battle, which the writer tells us was given by an eyewitness who he knew personally and thought was a reliable person. *Scalacronica* was written by the son of a participant in the battle, Sir Thomas Grey. Both father and son were professional soldiers who spent a great deal of their careers in Scotland, and Thomas junior tells us that he had access to Scottish material (which has not survived) while he was a prisoner of the Scots more than twenty years after the battle.

was not present at the battle himself, but his father (also Thomas) was taken prisoner during the first day of the fighting. The author was able to consult Scottish accounts, which have not survived, whilst he was himself a prisoner of war of the Scots a generation later. Additionally, unlike all of the other chroniclers, Grey was a professional soldier who spent most of his career fighting in Scotland; he is by far the closest thing we have to an expert witness.

All the narrative material is greatly enhanced if we examine the record material for the preceding twenty years or so. Pay rolls, horse valuations and other records can provide us with a better picture of the general military and social environment. Comprehending record evidence lets us understand the terms that the chroniclers use and failure to do so can lead us into serious errors. One example is the expression 'esquire'. To most people it means a young man aspiring to knighthood, and if he fought at all it was with lighter armour and a lighter horse than his knightly associate. In the fourteenth century it simply meant a man-at-arms, usually a landholder, who was not a knight. He was armed and mounted to the same standard and his role in battle was identical; in any force of heavy cavalry only a handful – perhaps 10 or 15 per cent at most – were actually knights. Failure to understand this has led to the invention of whole units of lightly armed gentry cavalry that exist only in the minds of modern writers.

Seven hundred years on from the battle, it is hardly surprising that we do not have all the evidence and information that we should like. In the absence of the 1314 pay rolls and muster rolls (which we can assume were lost on the battlefield), we can only make an educated guess about the numbers involved. This is less of an issue than it might appear since we have so much material – particularly about English armies – from campaigns in the years before and after 1314, from which we can make useful deductions. Army strengths are a thorny issue at the best of times and not necessarily especially useful information: nobody really knows exactly how many men fought at Waterloo in 1815 or on the Somme in 1916, but that does not have a significant impact on our understanding of either event. What matters more than a precise headcount is our ability to see a campaign or a battle in the round. If we have a decent understanding of the relative size of the forces involved, the arms and other equipment, the administrative practices of the day, the social and cultural ethos of the communities, and, most importantly, an understanding of how tactical practice was applied to the lie of the land, we will be far better informed than if we merely know that 20,000 men met 10,000 men in battle somewhere in the vicinity of a particular geographic feature.

As with any other battle – or indeed any event at all – the conclusions we come to today should not be set in stone. There is very little chance that a previously unknown contemporary eyewitness account of Bannockburn will come to light 700 years on, but if it did, it might completely alter our perception of the battle, even if it did not actually contradict any of the material

RECORD MATERIAL

As the name implies, this is evidence that we can find in Crown and other records of the day. There are several collections of such material from the later medieval period which can be accessed relatively easily through the inter-library loan scheme, including Bain's *Calendar of Documents Relating to Scotland*, Register of the Great Seal of Scotland and the Exchequer Rolls of Scotland.

we have today. Alternatively, it might invalidate a lot of the material we have now, but not change our understanding of the sequence of events; it certainly could not change the general outcome of the fighting: the Scots won and the English lost.

There is a greater possibility that scholars might uncover record evidence that would help to further our understanding. It is generally assumed – and probably correctly – that all of the English administrative records were lost on the battlefield, but it is not absolutely impossible that copies of pay rolls or other material may come to light and give us another glimpse into the structure or articulation of the army.

We can be a little more hopeful in regard to archaeology. The techniques of battlefield archaeology and the quality of interpretation are developing rapidly. There are currently plans for a major survey of the potential battle sites at Bannockburn and we may see a major breakthrough over the next few years which may compel historians to re-evaluate all of the record and narrative material that we have relied on in the past. Unfortunately, the soil in the Stirling area is not conducive to preserving organic material such as wood, cloth or leather, and is wet enough that ferrous (iron) artefacts are likely to have crumbled to dust long ago. Even so, traces of extensive numbers of fire hearths and the recovery of copper and brass objects or silver coins may yet provide us with some fresh data. Given the nature of the soil, it seems unlikely that the remains of the combatants will have survived, though clearly there were a great number of them, but it is quite possible that developments in soil analysis, geophysics or in the analysis of aerial photography may help to improve our comprehension of the battle.

Equally, we should be hopeful that in addition to archaeology, improvements in scholarship may develop our picture of the fighting. Until recent times this has not been a happy tale. The popular view of Bannockburn – indeed, of medieval war generally – bears little resemblance to what we actually know about it, and the fault for this can be laid fairly and squarely at the feet of scholars who, rather like the medieval chroniclers, have often had an agenda to pursue. Over a century ago, S.R. Gardiner and C.W.C. Oman (see Further Reading) developed a view of Bannockburn that fitted what they wanted to believe. They started with certain conclusions and accepted, enhanced or rejected – in some cases invented – evidence to suit those conclusions. Since that time many writers (including several who should have known better) have incorporated Oman or Gardiner's views into their own work. To this day, a writer can, with impunity, declare that Bannockburn was fought in bogs and swamps. Although all of the contemporary material is very clear that this was not the case, the bogs and swamps have become part of the 'received history' of Scotland and England.

Oman and Gardiner sought to establish a rationale for the mystery of Edward II's defeat, rather than searching for the roots of Robert I's victory. In fact, there is nothing very mysterious about Bannockburn. If we give due attention to the record and narrative material, we find that the battle was really a very straightforward affair and well within the 'norms' of medieval warfare.

TIMELINE

1286	Death of Alexander III
1290	Death of Margaret, Maid of Norway
1291–92	The Great Cause
1292	John Balliol inaugurated as King of Scotland
1295 October	Franco-Scottish treaty
1296 April	Edward I invades Scotland; the sack of Berwick
July	Edward deposes King John
1297 Spring	Rise of William Wallace
September	Battle of Stirling Bridge
1298 July	Battle of Falkirk
1303 February	Battle of Roslin
	Franco-English peace agreement
1304	Strathord Agreement
1306 March	Robert Bruce declares himself King of Scotland
June	Battle of Methven

1307		
April	Battle of Glentrool	
May	Battle of Loudoun Hill	
1308		
May	Battle of Inverurie	
1309	Robert I's first parliament held at	
March	St Andrews	
1312		
January	Robert I captures Perth	
1313		
October	Edward II announces invasion of Scotland	
1314		
March	Fall of Edinburgh to the Scots	
Lent	Earl of Carrick negotiates surrender pact for Stirling castle	
23/24		
June	Battle of Bannockburn	
1328	Treaty of Edinburgh-Northampton recognises Robert I as King of Scotland	

HISTORICAL
BACKGROUND

At the time of Alexander III's death in 1286, Scotland and England had enjoyed a long tradition of, essentially, good relations. Intermittent attempts by English kings over the preceding two centuries and more to procure a degree of sovereignty over their Scottish counterparts had never really taken root; indeed, it is questionable whether any English king had ever seriously believed that they would. William the Lion (reigned 1165–1214) was obliged to give homage for his kingdom after he was captured in 1174 as part of his ransom arrangements, but fifteen years later he paid a large sum to ensure that he and his successors would be free of any feudal obligation to the English Crown in the future. A century later, when Edward I came to the throne in England, the Scottish king, Alexander III, made a trip south to give homage for his various properties in England. Edward made a rather half-hearted attempt to have Scotland included in the homage ceremony, but this was robustly rejected by Alexander, who told him that the Kingdom of Scotland was held 'from God alone'[1], which Edward accepted and there the matter rested.

3. The coronation of Edward I. Edward only commanded one Scottish action in person, the Battle of Falkirk, 1298. His death in 1307 was a major blow to the fortunes of the English occupation forces, however the tide of the war had probably already started to turn in favour of the Scots.

Relations between the two countries were largely based on social relationships – cross-border landholding was fairly commonplace, but almost all of the properties were relatively modest. Although a Scottish lord might own several properties in England (or in France or Ireland), or vice versa, nobody was a top-ranking noble (or magnate) in both kingdoms. Naturally, any level of landholding automatically meant a degree of obligation to the Crown and therefore anyone who held land in both countries had a range of responsibilities to both kings, but this was never really a very serious problem before the English invasion of 1296, and its significance thereafter has been rather exaggerated by historians. The number of individuals involved

4. A sixteenth-century English artwork, depicting a fictitious parliament of Edward I attended by Llewellyn, Prince of Wales and Alexander III. Artworks and forged documents were an important weapon in the propaganda arsenals of medieval kings: the 'Dodgy Dossier' is not a modern innovation.

was not terribly large in either kingdom and the properties concerned were mostly quite modest. No individual held a property of greater significance than a barony in more than one kingdom. Contrary to the claims of many writers in the past, neither Robert Bruce, nor John Comyn or even Alexander III, was considered a magnate in the English political structure, though all three of them did hold valuable English properties.

There was surprisingly little economic activity between the two countries. England's trade lay mainly with France and Scotland's mainly with the Baltic and the Low Countries – the Netherlands and Belgium. Both countries depended on wool as the chief export crop and there was therefore little point in exporting wool from one to the other. There was, however, a considerable degree of cultural overlap. Both kingdoms had adopted the political and military ethos of France that we now call feudalism. In England this had come about through

BARONY

A form of landholding, baronies came in all shapes and sizes. Possession of a barony gave limited local government powers to the baron. The barony would be 'held' from the Crown in exchange for various obligations, usually an annual sum of money, though this was often a nominal payment. The chief responsibilities of the baron focused on maintaining law and order and the provision of a set number of men-at-arms for the king's army, and often, though not universally, providing infantry service as well. The baron would have the right to hold local courts, occasionally for capital crimes, and would collect rents and other sums (collectively known as the issues of the barony) from his tenants. Portions of the barony would generally be granted to other men who would, in exchange, provide the baron with the knight service he needed to fulfil his obligations to the Crown.

the Norman Conquest of 1066; in Scotland it had come about through a mixture of exposure to the practices of her southern neighbour, a considerable degree of intermarriage between the two royal families and the senior nobility, and the general adoption of 'feudal' practice across Northern and Western Europe. In short, that was how a 'modern' nation functioned in the later Middle Ages. Long before the outbreak of the wars of independence there was precious little practical cultural, military or political difference between most of Scotland and most of England. There were some very clear regional differences within both countries, but little or nothing to distinguish the social ethos of Brechin from that of Bedford, save that the average 'parish gentry' landholder in Bedford might be more likely to speak French – or at least be able to speak French – than his northern counterpart.

The generally cordial relationship between England and Scotland started to unravel with the death of Alexander III in March 1286. Alexander's two sons by his first marriage had already died, and his granddaughter Margaret (daughter of Erik II of Norway) had been recognised as his heir. There is a possibility that Alexander and Edward were planning a dynastic union of the two countries, which would be achieved by the marriage of Margaret to Edward's eldest son (the future Edward II), but Alexander, still only in his forties, married Yolande de Dreux in 1285 and clearly hoped to produce a direct heir. Alexander's death did not cause an immediate crisis. The Scottish political community was supportive, though the prospect of a female heir, especially one that was still a child, was certainly an unusual thing in medieval Europe. The political situation did, however, become a major issue when Margaret died en route to Scotland in 1290. There were now two serious claimants to the throne, John Balliol and Robert Bruce (grandfather of the man who would become Robert I), and a number of others who might make claims of more dubious validity. Since the death of Alexander, Scotland had been administered by a council of 'guardians' representing the major political groups in the community. This system had worked well for the intervening four years but the question of the succession was too momentous to be decided by a council of lords and clerics, and there was no prospect of reaching a unanimous agreement since the council contained supporters of both of the significant candidates. The council approached Edward I for advice, for which they have attracted a great deal of criticism from historians, but their actions were perfectly rational: Edward had had a good relationship with the late Alexander III; he was known to have a real interest in jurisprudence; he was powerful enough to impose the final decision if necessary; and he was acceptable to both of the main contenders. As the

5. John Balliol, from a Scottish amorial illuminated between 1581 and 1584. The king is surrounded by the broken symbols of his rule.

King of Scotland's only neighbour and a major player on the European political stage, he simply could not be ignored and if the process degenerated into a civil war – a real possibility – Edward might well allow the two sides to exhaust themselves and simply march into Scotland at the head of a great army and take over, as he had in Wales.

Edward was more than happy to take on the role, correctly identifying it as an opportunity to further his own interests in Scotland. The council did everything they reasonably could to ensure the future security of the realm, but Edward was an astute politician and would clearly have a strong negotiating position. He was not invited to arbitrate on the question of the succession. His role was to conduct a court of inquiry, ensure a fair and equitable process, and then oversee the installation of the successful candidate. In due course, a grand jury of 104 auditors was assembled. The auditors included forty chosen by John Balliol and forty chosen by Robert Bruce – a clear indication that none of the other candidates really had a serious case to present, but were simply making a demonstration of their interest in the event that both the Bruce and Balliol lines failed to produce heirs in the future. Edward was able to manipulate all of the candidates into accepting his overlordship as a condition of having their bids for the crown recognised at all. There was some resistance to this from various barons, but their position was undermined by the acceptance of Edward's demands by the different candidates. The case ran for over a year, but in November 1292 a decision was finally reached and John Balliol became King of Scotland, but was obliged to give homage for his realm to Edward.

Almost immediately, Edward's actions became increasingly overbearing. He asserted a right to hear appeals against John's court judgements and generally set about undermining John's authority at every opportunity. John was not in a position to challenge Edward's action and his political credibility suffered accordingly. Edward hoped to provoke John into open resistance and the opportunity arose when Edward issued writs demanding military service from John and various prominent members of the Scottish nobility for service against France.

At around this time, the majority of the Scottish political community had taken power out of John's hands. Initiatives of this nature were – to say the least – rare in medieval politics, but the process was eased by the fact that a committee of guardians

6. Illuminated capital from an English medieval document depicting a scene from the siege of Carlisle.

had ruled effectively during the years between the death of Alexander III and the death of his granddaughter Margaret: a period of four years. The Scottish political community had acquired some experience of governing a kingdom without actually having a king; experience that would prove invaluable in the years between 1297 and 1304.

The new council made a treaty of mutual defence with the King of France. And from 1295 there was, in theory at least, a state of war between England and Scotland. In practice, very little happened. Edward was already busy with his war in France and was unable to pursue operations in Scotland until the spring of 1296. Both sides raised armies, but the Scots simply had no idea about how to conduct a war. There had not been war in Scotland for more than thirty years, and that had been a relatively short affair that had been dealt with by the county communities of the south-west. Edward, on the other hand, was an experienced commander who pursued his campaign with purpose. The Scots made some rather purposeless raids into northern England, but Edward approached the town of Berwick, stormed it and sacked the community with enormous loss of life. The town – in those days one of the most significant commercial centres in the British Isles – was largely destroyed, but Edward effectively sent a signal to every other town in Scotland: resistance was not only futile, since hardly any Scottish towns had defences of any kind, let alone serious fortification, but would also result in the utter destruction of the community. There was only one action in the rest of the 1296 campaign. A body of Scottish men-at-arms encountered a similar English force near Dunbar and were completely routed. Only one fatality is recorded, but in the fighting and the subsequent surrender of Dunbar castle more than 200 members of the Scottish nobility and gentry were taken prisoner. The main body of the Scottish army, now

7. The obverse and reverse of the seal of Edward I.

bereft of leadership and purpose, simply dissolved and made their way home without ever seeing action.

The Scottish government had not enjoyed the full support of the political community. One, Robert Bruce (grandson of the man who had sought to become king in 1291–92), had sided with Edward I in the hope that his father (his grandfather had died in the interim) would now be installed on the throne at the hands of Edward I. He was quickly disabused of this; Edward had no plans to make anybody King of Scotland, least of all Robert Bruce. Instead, Edward marched northwards demanding homage and the surrender of castles and towns, all of which was easily accomplished, given the events at Berwick. By July he had captured John, forced his abdication and packed him off to London as a prisoner. Assuming – perhaps understandably – that the war was won, Edward left the consolidation of an occupation administration to his lieutenants and returned to the more pressing affairs at home.

The Scots had certainly been defeated and Edward had obliged a great number of Scottish nobles and towns to give homage, but recovery was rapid. Within a matter of months, Edward's officers reported that the Scots were in the process of forming a government and were appointing officials in many areas, and that only two counties – Berwickshire and Roxburgh – were under occupation control and they 'only lately'[2]. Any hopes that Edward had of imposing his own rule quickly and securely disappeared in early 1297. One of the prisoners taken the previous year, Sir Andrew Murray, escaped from captivity, made his way back to the north-east of Scotland and raised a force which set siege to strongholds. Robert Bruce had decided to jump ship and was assembling a force in the west, while William Wallace, youngest son of an obscure Ayrshire knight, was conducting operations in central Scotland.

Bruce was now fighting for King John, though he had been conspicuous by his absence the previous year. In practice, if he ever wanted to be king himself, Bruce had to be seen as espousing the cause of independence. For Wallace and Murray the matter was more clear-cut: they were simply fighting to get John restored to the throne. Due to his commitments elsewhere, Edward was unable to take to the field himself and entrusted operations in Scotland to his lieutenants. The 'noble revolt' of Bruce and others was resolved through negotiations at Irvine, though there was a strong suspicion that he dragged the discussions out as long as he could to allow Wallace and Murray more time to gather and train their troops. True or not, by the time Sir Hugh Cressingham – Edward's treasurer for Scotland – was able to get to Stirling, he found that Murray and Wallace had combined their forces on the north bank of the river. Confident that his force was more than a match for anything the Scots might have to offer, Cressingham tried to cross the river and was soundly defeated.

Wallace and Murray were now effectively masters of Scotland north of the River Forth and throughout much of the south. They acted as guardians in the name of King John, but Murray died a few weeks after the battle – possibly of wounds incurred in the action – leaving Wallace in sole charge. It was rare indeed for someone of such lowly political status to acquire so much power, but there was something of a political vacuum. Some of the more prominent lords had already been neutralised at Irvine; some simply wanted a quiet life and were prepared to accept Edward's lordship; some – particularly in the south-east, where they were most vulnerable to English military power – were hesitant to resist; but, most significantly, a large number were still prisoners of war following the debacle of the 1296 campaign.

At about this time, Edward freed a number of senior figures – notably Sir John Comyn, Lord of Badenoch – to serve in his army in Flanders in exchange for their liberty, only to have them defect and escape to France at the earliest opportunity and then return to Scotland to continue the fight.

Clearly Edward had to act if he was to achieve his goals in Scotland, but he was unable to bring an army to the field until the late summer of 1298. By this time most of Scotland was under Wallace's control and initially Edward struggled to come to grips with his opponent. Just as he was on the verge of running out of money and supplies to keep his army in existence, Edward was able to steal a march on Wallace and inflicted a major defeat on him at Falkirk. Since Wallace's political authority had depended entirely on his military credibility, he was swiftly ousted from the position of guardian and his place was taken by Bruce and Comyn. This was not a happy arrangement. The Comyns had an excellent track record as servants of the Crown and were closely associated with King John, but Bruce had been on the English side in 1296 and clearly had royal ambitions of his own. Despite their differences, Comyn and Bruce managed their campaign reasonably effectively. In the aftermath of Falkirk, Edward had been obliged to leave Scotland once again to tend to concerns elsewhere and may even have believed that the

Scottish situation was now largely settled and could be left to his subordinates.

This was clearly not the case. In 1299 – at the behest of the pope and as part of negotiations with France – Edward had released John Balliol, and by 1300 there seemed to be a real possibility that he might be restored to the throne. This was not an attractive proposition to Robert Bruce, who now made his peace with Edward, abandoning the Balliol cause. Despite his defection, the Scots continued to make headway, but Edward could not make an opportunity to take matters into his own hands until he had reached a satisfactory conclusion in France. Eventually he was able to force a peace treaty which specifically excluded the Scots and secured a statement in which King John rejected any further involvement in Scottish affairs.

The loss of France as an ally was a body blow to the Scots, and since John was no longer interested in his own restoration, it was now difficult for his supporters to be clear about what they were fighting for. Additionally, Edward now brought a large army to Scotland, but also made it clear that he was prepared to negotiate terms. In February 1304, an agreement was reached at Strathord and the war came to an end. For Edward this was a very important achievement. Aware that he was nearing the end of his life, he was eager to finish his Scottish business, but it is not at all clear that he really believed he had secured his authority. At least a proportion of the Scots seem to have seen the Strathord Agreement as more of an armistice than a final settlement, and a few prominent figures – notably William Wallace – were specifically excluded from the terms and were thus still active in the field. In August 1305, Wallace was captured, subjected to a travesty of a trial and executed.

The exclusion of Wallace and a few others was, to some extent, a matter of public relations. The garrison of Stirling castle – which had also been specifically excluded from the

Strathord terms – held out for some time, declaring that they were not fighting for Balliol's kingship, but for 'The Lion' (the heraldic symbol of the nation), but with no prospect of relief their resistance was probably more to do with seeking honourable terms than anything else. Wallace was a different matter. The Scottish war had been a heavy burden on Edward's kingdom and someone had to carry the can and satisfy English public opinion for 'rebellion'. Overall, the execution of Wallace – and the manner of it – was an unwise move on the part of Edward. Wallace was, by this time, politically insignificant, but deliberate persecution made Edward look petty and the elaborate executions were not part of the general ethos of medieval Scotland. Had Edward simply imprisoned him, Wallace would probably have fallen out of public consciousness along with the other men who had resisted the occupation and are now known only to a handful of medieval scholars and enthusiasts.

Although he felt a need to make an example and perhaps demonstrate a degree of closure to his Scottish wars, Edward could not afford to impose too heavy a settlement on the Scottish magnates and the wider political community. If he was to rule successfully he needed their support to run the country. It was clear that he could not simply execute all of the nobles who had fought against him and replace them with English lords. There were not enough candidates and such a policy would inevitably breed hostility; moreover, he could not possibly execute all the sons, cousins and nephews of Scottish lords who might at some point rebel to recover their lost heritages, and who would very likely be able to gather support from the community quite easily. Edward had not made sweeping changes to administrative or legal practices in Scotland – the only law he abolished was the 'law of the Scots and the Brets' which had been in desuetude for generations – but his occupation government was seen as oppressive and, inevitably, foreign. It is important to remember that in the Middle Ages England and Scotland were as much different countries as Portugal and France. This may have been rather lost on Edward himself, since there was a good deal of common practice in both kingdoms.

His general intention toward Scotland is less than clear. He made no effort to incorporate Scotland formally into England, nor did he arrange to have himself officially declared as king. It is possible that he hoped to achieve a situation in which Scotland would be a spate lordship owned by the English Crown, but not subject to interference by the English parliament, and he seems to have had no intention of calling a Scottish parliament. Instead he set up a council of magnates – mostly Scottish – and entrusted administration to them. Edward may have genuinely believed that the death of Wallace was the final act in the conquest of Scotland, though that would have been a rather optimistic assessment. Realistically there were at least two possible sources of contention. One was Robert Bruce, who was certainly in Edward's peace but is most unlikely to have given up on his regal ambitions at any point. The other was Edward Balliol, son of the deposed King John. John's deposition and abdication had been forced at the point of the sword and was therefore easily recognisable as an act of coercion by a greater military power. Medieval legal practice understood the concept of duress and John's abdication was thus invalid in itself. In 1303 he had surrendered all his rights in Scottish matters, but it was, at best, questionable as to whether he could legally discard the claims of his legitimate heir. Edward Balliol was still young and in due course might well attempt to restore the family line. The Scottish political establishment was rather conservative and if Edward Balliol could bring any sort of a force to Scotland there was every chance that he would be

PEELS

Edward I constructed a number of peels in the late 1290s and early 1300s. A peel was not really a castle, but was more purely a military establishment. Most of the peels were major installations with powerful garrisons containing a mobile striking force of several scores of men-at-arms who could be committed to actions in support of castles in the vicinity, though the peel at Linlithgow was a very small affair with only a handful of archers and men-at-arms.

able to gather widespread support since he was, after all, the legitimate heir to the throne.

Through the autumn and winter of 1305/06, there seems to have been no serious opposition to Edward's rule in Scotland. The royal castles, and some baronial ones, were garrisoned and work continued on the construction of a number of peels, though not with any great sense of urgency. The garrisons were mostly quite small and, all in all, there was a brief period of peace, but the situation was far from settled. Robert Bruce was still determined to acquire the throne and in February 1306 he met with his chief political rival, John Comyn. According to the poet John Barbour, writing more than half a century after the event, Bruce offered to grant all of his property – most significantly the Earldom of Carrick and the Lordship of Annandale – to Comyn in exchange for unequivocal support for Bruce's kingship. Alternatively, Bruce would give his support to Comyn in exchange for all of the great Comyn lordships of the north-east. Barbour's account is, at best, suspect in this regard. The Bruce claim to the throne was weaker than that of the Balliols, but he would certainly be the next legitimate heir to the throne if the Balliol line was excluded; the Comyn family, however, had no legal claim to the throne at all. Regardless, the

8. Significant towns and castles in late medieval Scotland.

two men met at Dumfries for some purpose, and it is almost certain that they were planning to take action against the occupation. The Comyns' long tradition of loyal service to the Crown would suggest that John Comyn favoured a coup that would, in due course, put Edward Balliol on the throne, but that might be a threat to the Bruce family, since they had not supported John's kingship in 1296 and had only fought for him intermittently thereafter.

Whatever the motivation and whatever offers were made, the meeting was a disaster for the Bruce party. Robert – or one of his supporters – killed John Comyn at the altar of the Greyfriars and thereby started a ferocious blood feud between the two families. It is a reasonable assumption that Bruce was planning to make a move anyway, but the death of Comyn forced his hand. He tried to communicate with Edward, but was rebuffed, and on Palm Sunday 1306 he had himself inaugurated as King of Scotland. Less than a year after the end of Wallace's resistance to Edward, there was war once again. Robert would probably have preferred to wait for a better opportunity. Edward was old and ill, and could not be expected to live much longer; furthermore his heir – Edward of Carnarvon – was seen as being less assiduous than his father and not such a potent adversary.

Robert's campaign started badly. He was able to gather a considerable degree of support from the political community, but this was offset by the fact that the Comyn family and their allies were vehemently opposed to him and by the fact that he was not really the legitimate heir. By early summer, Bruce had gathered something of an army, but he was not yet a very competent commander. On 19 June his troops were attacked and scattered in a dawn attack at Methven by a force under Sir Aymer de Valence, Earl of Pembroke and brother-in-law to the late John Comyn. Bruce moved to the west in search of further support while sending his queen – Elizabeth de Burgh – into the north-east to take sanctuary at Tain. A second defeat at the hand of John of Lorne reduced him to being no more than the leader of a party of bandits, and for the next several months Robert disappears from record. It is generally believed that he sought and found shelter in the Western Isles; Edward ordered a party to seek him out on the island of Rathlin, off the coast of Ireland, and some writers have made a case that Robert travelled to Orkney or Shetland, or even to Norway. In his absence, Edward was able to restore his own authority across much of the country and a number of Bruce's early supporters came to Edward's peace, either because they were disillusioned with the Bruce cause or because they feared for their estates or even their lives.

The latter was unmistakeably a serious consideration. Robert's queen and his daughter by his first marriage (Marjory) fell into Edward's hands and were imprisoned, but his brother Neil was executed. The same fate might have befallen Elizabeth, but her father was the Earl of Ulster, a powerful Irish magnate and a crucial part of Edward's Irish administration. He could not afford to alienate the earl, but equally he could not afford to release Elizabeth, lest she escape to Scotland and provide Robert with a male heir. Executing his existing heir, Marjory, would have been barbaric in the extreme, besides which she could potentially prove useful in the future. If Edward succeeded in destroying Robert Bruce, he might at some point put a favourable face on appointing a replacement Earl of Carrick by marrying her off to his new appointee.

Robert returned to the stage in February 1307. He organised two attacks in the south-west. One party under himself and his younger brother Edward made a landing at Turnberry, which was less than successful, but the other under his brothers Thomas and Alexander landed at Loch Ryan and was thoroughly defeated. Like Neil, Thomas and Alexander were executed without trial, which was a clear political statement on the part of Edward. In future, his opponents in Scotland could not expect to be treated with the normal usages of medieval warfare: there would be no ransoms or imprisonment, just death sentences. Edward adhered to this policy for a while, but it had to be abandoned some time before the close of 1308 due to the increasing number of English prisoners in Scottish custody.

Edward's death at Burgh-on-the-Sands in 1307, when he was en route to yet another campaign in Scotland, passed the problem to his son, Edward II. The new king was not happy about the Scottish situation, but he had many other issues to deal with, not least his coronation, a major financial crisis and a difficult relationship with France, and was unable to focus his attention on Scotland. Edward's problems helped to ease the course of the Bruce party. Despite the major setbacks of the first year and more of his reign, by the summer of 1308 he had defeated most of his internal opponents, acquired political control over much of the northern part of Scotland and was starting to make serious inroads against the occupation government. His approach differed considerably from the policies adopted by Wallace and Murray, and from the guardianship in which he had taken an active role. He made no attempt to hold on to the castles that he captured. Doing so would have depleted the strength of his field army and any castle that was later recaptured and garrisoned by the English would put a dent in his credibility, so instead he slighted them. He did not actually destroy them, which would have taken a good deal of time and effort, but he tore down gate defences and breached walls to make them indefensible without a major programme of reconstruction, for which Edward could afford neither the manpower nor the money.

In the summer of 1310, Edward II was at last able to mount a significant campaign aimed at reinstating the ground lost to the

Bruce party and, if possible, bringing Robert to battle. Little, if anything, was achieved, though the cost was considerable both financially and in terms of Edward's prestige and credibility. He failed utterly to force a major engagement and by the end of the year, having run out of money and with his army melting away through desertion, Edward had retired to Berwick, where he would spend the next six months or so. The campaign was a failure for Edward, but was inevitably a propaganda coup for Robert. Two months after Edward left Berwick to attend to his domestic issues, Robert took an army into Tynedale, where they seized considerable sums of money and vast numbers of cattle.

A month later he mounted a second expedition into Northumberland. Unlike similar raids by Wallace in 1297, Robert's force did not indulge in looting and pillaging. Instead, Robert demanded – and received – the enormous sum of £2,000 from the community of Northumberland in exchange for a truce until February 1312. The funds gathered allowed Robert to pay his troops instead of allowing them to plunder, but the absence of destruction meant that he would be able to demand similar sums in the future and, just as usefully, demand free passage into more southerly counties which would be subjected to the same treatment in the years to come.

At the end of 1311, Robert had gained complete control of Scotland north of the River Forth with the exceptions of the towns and castles of Perth and Dundee. The first fell to a night attack in January 1312, when a visiting French knight was surprised – even horrified – to see Robert himself strip off and swim through the cold water of the Tay to take part in the operation. Dundee fell later in the year, possibly through a surrender pact.

By the end of the year Robert's credibility had grown to the point where modest numbers of landholders in central counties like Lothian, Fife and Clackmannanshire, which were still more or less under English control, were starting to enter his peace despite the risks to their estates should he be defeated. Clearly the war had swung in his favour and there was less belief that Edward was capable of re-imposing his government in Scotland. There was greater opposition elsewhere. Many of the gentry and aristocracy of Roxburghshire, Berwickshire, Lothian and Dumfriesshire served in English garrisons; some for wages and some because they were obliged to discharge the military obligations attached to their landholding or face forfeiture. And, of course, there was still the matter of Robert's legitimacy as king. So long as the Balliol line survived, John – and, after his death, his son Edward – would continue to be the legitimate king and Robert would continue to be a usurper.

All the same, success draws support and by the summer of 1313 even Lothian was only nominally under occupation rule as greater numbers of the political community turned to the Bruce party, in part at least because Robert was now forcing them to make the same sort of payments for peace that he had forced on the community of Northumberland, and partly because the Bruce party was increasingly seen as being in a better position to provide an environment of steady law and order. That perception was encouraged by the behaviour of some of the occupation garrisons, who had taken to seizing goods and money from local inhabitants – even those who had been supportive of the occupation government over several years.

Edward had not, however, abandoned his hopes for a recovery. In an exercise that smacks strongly of political stage management, the justiciar (chief judge) of Lothian, Sir Adam Gordon, petitioned Edward to come to the aid of his loyal subjects in Scotland. Edward's response was to announce a major offensive for the following summer. At this juncture the great castles of southern and central Scotland were not yet seen as being at risk, though the great peel may have fallen to the Scots at about this time. Clearly Edward hoped to restore his Scottish administration by military means. If he could bring about a major battle and defeat Robert, he would have taken a major step in that direction. A similar policy had, superficially, been successful against William Wallace in 1298; however, the Battle of Falkirk – though a major victory – had really achieved little more than the replacement of Wallace as guardian. It had not brought about a collapse of the Scottish resistance, which in fact continued to prosper – even the great castle of Stirling fell to the Balliol party in 1299. In fact, Edward had little choice but to make a major demonstration, though he had problems enough at home already. Failure to have pursued the war with the Scots would have reflected badly on his own abilities as king. He would have been seen as abandoning his father's achievements, though in reality Edward I had failed to bring his Scottish wars to a satisfactory conclusion. He had to show some commitment to those Scots who had accepted his kingship, many of whom were now pensioners of the English Crown and living in exile, as well as those who continued to support his kingship in the southern counties, especially in Lothian, Roxburghshire, Berwickshire and Dumfriesshire. He also had to support the claims of those English who had been granted lands and offices in Scotland by himself or by his father, or who – like Henry de Beaumont – had claims to estates that had been declared forfeit by King Robert.

Edward's plans seem to have had little or no effect on the Bruce party. King Robert's forces continued to press on with the campaign. Although the most obvious sign of their success was the capture of castles and towns, the Bruce party's progress was really more a matter of expanding the area under Robert's control, and by the end of 1313, even in those areas where the garrisons still held out, there was very little of the occupation to rescue. The castles were still manned, but they seem to have become isolated outposts holding out against the enemy rather than active garrisons imposing Edward's administration in the localities. The early months of 1314 did nothing to improve the position. In February and March the castles of Roxburgh and Edinburgh fell to forces under Douglas and the Earl of Moray respectively, thus effectively compromising the ability of the remaining strongholds to support one another. By Lent the garrison of Stirling was under close siege from the Earl of Carrick, and this is what forced the hand of the constable of the castle – Sir Philip Moubray – to make a surrender pact with the earl. Criticism of both parties rather fails to take account of the reality of the situation. Given the time of year, Moubray's supply situation must have been poor at best and perilous at worst for both the men and the horses of the garrison. His stores would have become depleted through the winter; even if he had acquired massive quantities of hay in the autumn of 1313, the horses of the men-at-arms would have consumed at least the greater part of it by March and he could not hope to replenish it whilst under siege. By making the pact, Moubray was able to ensure that his men would not be either starved into surrender or killed in a siege that he could not hope to withstand indefinitely. Equally, although it is easy to assume that Carrick was simply bored with conducting a siege, this is a supposition based on Barbour's view of Carrick as a rather flighty sort of man. In fact, the pact allowed Carrick to conduct more immediately useful operations elsewhere. Since King Edward was already committed to a major invasion of Scotland in the summer of 1314, it made no real difference whether Stirling castle remained in English hands until starved out or stormed, or whether the garrison held out until the arrival of Edward's army.

To some extent the threat of losing the castle possibly encouraged Edward to make Stirling his initial objective, but the key word is 'initial'. He had to do more than simply take an army to Scotland and inflict a defeat – even a crushing defeat – on the Scots. He would have to lead his forces throughout Scotland if he was to successfully re-impose his government. If the castle fell and was then recovered after a successful battle, it would only be one fortress among many that would require extensive repair and renovation. Stirling was certainly a key location in the sense that a powerful garrison there could control movement across the Forth, but it was no more significant politically than Edinburgh in the south or Aberdeen in the north. If the occupation was to be effective, it needed to have control of the major towns and castles, but there was no value to that unless the garrisons were able to operate in the wider community. They had to be able to do more than just collect rents and taxes, control law and order and extract military service; they had to be able to prevent anybody else from competing for authority.

NOTES
1 J. Stevenson, *Documents Illustrative of Scottish History*
2 Ibid.

THE ARMIES

The Commanders

Edward II

Edward has carried a great weight of hostility for 700 years, which is rather less than just. He had accrued quite an extensive experience of campaigning against the Scots, though he had never been able to bring them to battle. He has been widely criticised for not carrying out his father's wishes and pursuing the campaign on which Edward I died in 1307, but as a new king he had more than enough issues to deal with at that moment – not least the enormous debts that his father had incurred in a decade of unsuccessful wars in Scotland. In 1307, Robert I was still little more than a brigand in the hills with very limited overt support and a great deal of opposition from those who were prepared to accept the Plantagenets and from the rather greater proportion of the population who still favoured the return of the Balliol line. However much Edward might have wanted to pursue his Scottish affairs, his immediate priorities lay elsewhere. He might have enjoyed greater success if he had pursued his campaign against Robert more assiduously in 1308–11, but he had to face extensive opposition from his own nobility as well as dealing with the situation in France. By the end of 1312 he had managed to overcome a significant part of his domestic political difficulties, but by this point Robert had become sufficiently powerful that only a major campaign was likely to dislodge him. In 1314, Edward had a staff of talented and experienced officers, all of whom were taken just as much by surprise at the dawn attack of Robert I as Edward was.

Aymer de Valence, Earl of Pembroke

A competent and experienced soldier and a valued diplomat, de Valence had had mixed fortunes in Scotland. He had defeated Robert at Methven in 1306 only to be beaten in turn at Loudoun Hill a year later. He was, in general, a loyal and effective servant of both Edward I and Edward II. He was one of the 'Lords Ordainer' rebels who tried to exert control over what they saw as Edward II's excesses, but aligned himself with the king after the Ordainers executed Piers Gaveston. De Valence was able to extract himself and a considerable body of troops from the defeat at Bannockburn.

Sir Robert Clifford

Clifford spent a very considerable part of his career in Scotland. He was present at the Irvine negotiations that ended the 'noble revolt' of 1297 and at the Battle of Falkirk the following year. From 1308 he was Edward II's chief officer in Scotland, but was unable to prevent King Robert from gaining control over most of the country. Clifford was killed in action at Bannockburn and his body was sent home to be buried at Shap Abbey.

Gilbert de Clare, Earl of Gloucester

A grandson of Edward I, Gloucester was active in the Scottish wars and held significant posts in the occupation army. He held a senior command at Bannockburn and was, arguably, the most prominent of the English casualties. According to Barbour, King Robert held a vigil over Gloucester's body, which was returned to England for burial at Tewkesbury Abbey.

Humphrey de Bohun, Earl of Hereford

De Bohun was less than happy about his status within the army. As marshal of England, he felt – understandably – that he should have had a more prominent position. He managed to escape capture at Bannockburn and fled to Bothwell castle, where he was admitted and then promptly taken prisoner when the commander of the castle learned of the defeat of the English army.

Sir Henry de Beaumont

Definitely one of the most outstanding career soldiers of his day, de Beaumont served Edward I in Flanders and then extensively in Scotland, losing his horse at Falkirk. He had a vested interest in defeating Bruce since he had married Alice, heir to John Comyn, Earl of Buchan, and claimed the earldom in right of his wife. He was a leading figure in the attempt to put Edward Balliol on the Scottish throne in 1332 and should probably be credited with developing the classic longbow tactic, which was first used at Dupplin Muir. Beaumont escaped from Bannockburn with Edward II.

Sir Giles d'Argentan

Sir Giles was not, strictly speaking, one of the commanders, but he was one of the most prominent paladins of the age. Entrusted with the security of King Edward II, he ensured that the king escaped from the battlefield and then returned to the fight and was killed in action.

Sir Henry de Bohun

De Bohun was not one of the more significant commanders, but was definitely one of the more famous names. Immediately before the first engagement at the New Park, de Bohun (a nephew of Humphrey de Bohun, Earl of Hereford) saw an opportunity to acquire great fame and status by killing Robert in single combat. The duel did not have the outcome that Sir Henry expected, since King Robert killed him with a single stroke of an axe, but he certainly got his name into the history books.

Robert I

Within weeks of declaring himself king, Robert was roundly defeated by Aymer de Valence at Methven, near Perth. The following year started badly for the Bruce cause, with a landing in the south-west and the capture of two of Robert's brothers, both of whom were executed by Edward I in a fit of pique.

By the end of 1307, Robert had come to grips with his situation and was soon making steady, if unspectacular progress. Initially he was very dependent on troops from the Hebrides and West Highlands furnished by Angus Og and other Celtic lords, possibly including Christina MacRuarie, who was rumoured to have become his mistress. These western potentates had largely escaped the attentions of Edward I, but were now concerned that the relative independence they had enjoyed in the past might be threatened and that their future would be more secure under the rule of a Scottish king than an English one.

Robert's first significant victories against the occupation forces – at Glentrool and Loudoun Hill – were not large actions, but they did give him a degree of credibility and by 1308 he was in a position to take on his internal opposition, primarily the Comyn family. The Comyns had a long track record as loyal and effective supporters of the Crown and had only given up the fight against Edward I in 1304, when the country was in a state of physical and financial exhaustion. Even at that point, it is not absolutely clear that they had really finally accepted the suzerainty of Edward I, but rather that they viewed the Strathord Agreement more as an armistice and might well take up arms again on behalf of the Balliol cause, if not for King John, then possibly for his son Edward, who was now approaching an age when he could take an active role in his own right. Robert had had a tempestuous relationship with the Comyns and had finally destroyed any prospect of gaining their support by his murder of John Comyn, Lord of Badenoch, at the Greyfriars, Dumfries, in February 1306. This was an act that likely propelled Robert to seize the crown rather earlier than he had planned. A series of campaigns in the north-east and the south-west, and his ability to force the Earl of Ross to accept his authority, gave Robert control over a great deal of Scotland; in 1309 he was able to hold his first recorded parliament at St Andrews. His enemy, Edward II, had more than enough troubles of his own and was

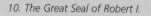

9. A silver penny of Robert I. Pennies of a given weight and purity of silver were known as 'sterlings' (a term that originated from Germany) and were acceptable right across Europe.

10. The Great Seal of Robert I.

unable to prevent Robert from forcing truces, which allowed him to consolidate his administration across most of the country and then, from 1311 onward, to mount increasingly ambitious raids into England, demanding ransoms and free passage from communities in Northumberland and Cumbria.

Although Edward II mounted expeditions into Scotland, his forces failed to force Robert to offer battle and one by one the remaining English-held strongholds fell to the Scots. In 1312, Dundee was surrendered – possibly through a surrender compact similar to the one procured by Edward Bruce at Stirling in 1314. With the fall of Edinburgh and Roxburgh in the late winter and spring of 1314, only Stirling, Berwick and Bothwell remained in English hands. Bothwell was not a particularly important castle, but Berwick and Stirling were significant strongholds; however, in both cases the garrisons were unable to fulfil their main function – the imposition of government – and were no more than isolated outposts in a country most of which was firmly in the Bruce camp.

Edward Bruce, Earl of Carrick

As Robert's sole surviving brother, Edward Bruce was his closest male heir and naturally held a significant position in the Bruce cause, but he was also a competent and assiduous soldier, leading a successful campaign to bring Galloway under Bruce control.

In Barbour's narrative, Carrick's decision to make a surrender pact with Sir Philip Moubray was a major factor in bringing about a battle at Stirling and rashly gave Edward II a whole year to prepare his invasion. In reality, the pact was agreed at Lent in 1314, not 1313, and therefore was to last for only three months, and Edward had been committed to a major invasion of Scotland since the previous October, if not before. Pacts of this nature were normal practice in medieval warfare. Moubray was well aware that Edward intended to bring an army to Stirling before midsummer and the Bruce party seem to have been fairly well informed about decisions at Edward II's court, so Carrick was probably aware of the plan as well. The pact suited both parties since the garrison would no longer be under threat and could purchase supplies in the town while the besiegers could move off to undertake other projects.

Thomas Randolph, Earl of Moray

A nephew of Robert I, Sir Thomas had been one of his earliest supporters but had defected to the Plantagenet cause after being captured at the Battle of Methven in 1306. He was taken prisoner by King Robert's forces in 1308 and sometime thereafter renewed his allegiance to Robert. He served his king well and soon became one of his principal lieutenants. In 1312, Robert resurrected the title of Earl of Moray and bestowed it on Randolph, thus giving him the resources and authority to bring the north-east firmly under Bruce control and fatally undermining the prestige of the Comyn family. Moray seized Edinburgh castle in a daring night attack in March 1314 and commanded the action near St Ninian's chapel on 23 June, and a division of the army on the following day.

Sir James Douglas

Although Douglas would eventually become one of the great military figures of the age with a reputation across the whole of Europe, in 1314 his star was still in ascendance. He had yet to become a figure of any great political significance. His father, William 'le Hardi', had resisted Edward I in the early stages of the conflict. He had been captured and forfeited of the Barony of Douglas in Lanarkshire, which Edward granted to Sir Robert Clifford. Educated in Paris, he returned to Scotland in the household of William Lamberton, Bishop of St Andrews. In 1304, he asked Edward I for the return of the family property that had been forfeited by his father, but was refused. Concluding that the prospects of restoration to the family estate were better with the Bruce party, Douglas joined King Robert and acquired a reputation as a great warrior.

Barbour accords Douglas a major role in the main battle at Bannockburn, claiming that the Scots deployed in four divisions, one of which was commanded jointly by Douglas and Walter the Stewart. Barbour had two agendas to pursue in doing this. Since Douglas was such a great figure to Barbour's audience, it was almost unthinkable that he would not have a significant command role, and Barbour duly obliged. Equally, Barbour's patron was Robert II, grandson of Robert I and the son of Walter. By ascribing an important position to the Stewart and associating him so closely with Douglas, Barbour effectively secured the approval of his benefactor. Douglas continued to enhance his reputation after Bannockburn. He led the pursuit of Edward II to Dunbar, conducted several campaigns in England and very nearly captured Edward III during the Weardale campaign of 1327.

Sir Robert Keith, Earl Marischal

Captured in a small action on the River Cree in 1300, Sir Robert was released under the terms of the Strathord Agreement in 1304. By 1308 he was firmly in the Bruce camp, though his property lay in areas under English control. As Earl Marischal he commanded the Scottish cavalry at Bannockburn and undertook various diplomatic tasks for the king in the years after the battle. He was killed in action at Dupplin Muir in 1332.

11. The memorial of Angus Og, Lord of the Isles. Although he was a vital supporter of Robert I's kingship from 1307 onward, it is not clear whether he was present at Bannockburn.

The Soldiers

What we know of other English armies of the time would indicate that a substantial proportion of the troops were drafted rather than volunteers and that some served to avoid criminal prosecution or paying fines, but we should not equate that with crude criminality such as robbery, but with a wide variety of shortcomings including tax avoidance or failure to perform some civic duty. Men of all social ranks served to procure pardons for their failings and in some cases men would join the army to procure 'protections' – Crown documents which allowed them to avoid court actions being raised in their absence.

Military service was certainly a duty for virtually every male in an emergency, but planned armies – like those of 1314 – were largely drawn from the classes that could afford the money to equip themselves and the time to train, and who owed stipulated military obligations to the Crown or to a feudal superior.

Almost every modern description of the Battle of Bannockburn lists troop types which are assumed, rather than demonstrated, to have been present, or in some cases – like the lightly armed young squire – only exist through a failure to understand the nature of fourteenth-century military terms and practices. Foremost amongst these are the 'small folk' of Barbour's poem. We should not discard the idea of their existence; far from it. The Scottish army, like any other, would have had a large number of farriers, blacksmiths, armourers, fletchers, bowyers, grooms and other tradesmen vital to the

Opposite: 12. Detail from a Scottish grave effigy showing a fourteenth-century soldier with bascinet, padded jack and the 'heater'-shaped shield typical of the period.

CALTROPS

A caltrop was fashioned from two or three short lengths of iron to form a four-pointed object – generally between 2in and 4in tall – which would present a vertical spike whichever way up it landed and thus be a threat to unwary soldiers, particularly mounted men. Although a few caltrops have allegedly been 'recovered' from the Bannockburn area, it is clear that all of them (so far) have been the product of local blacksmiths hoping to make some money by 'finding' caltrops and selling them to visitors.

operational capacity of the fighting men. There would also have been large numbers of camp servants, cooks and a host of other personnel, some of whom would have had assistants. There would undoubtedly have been a considerable number of 'hangers-on' with no particular role or skill, but who had attached themselves to the army in the hope that there would be pickings of some kind in due course. It would be more than just strange if these men – and we should assume that they would mostly be men – were to witness a successful battle and not seize the opportunity to descent to the field in the hope of acquiring some sort of booty or perhaps even a prisoner they would be able to ransom. They might even be seized with the excitement of the moment and a touch of blood lust and rush to the battlefield, but it is clear from those accounts closer to the event than Barbour that the 'small folk' played no part in King Robert's victory. One of the weaknesses of trying to find a place for every piece of information available from chronicles is the danger of adding items to the narrative that are clearly not valid. The chronicler Bower tells us that the English army included slingers and brought caltrops, though no contemporary material indicates

13. An assemblage of plate armour to protect the arm. Pieces as sophisticated as this one were still relatively rare in 1314 and would have been very much the province of the wealthy or of men who spent a large proportion of their time in military service.

slingers for this battle any more than for any other campaign of the wars of independence. Even so, numerous accounts of the action have not only included slingers, but maps have been produced to show their location on the field. Curiously, although Bower also tells us that the English army was equipped with bombards, no writer has found a place for them in the narrative, though they have just as much prominence as the slingers or the caltrops.

The same question of inclusion of every point of evidence also arises for such observations and deductions as we might make from record evidence drawn from other campaigns of the same period. The fact that certain troops are not described as taking part does not mean that they were absent, though it's a reasonable assumption that if they were not mentioned they did not have a significant impact on the course of the fighting. Other English expeditionary forces in the fourteenth century certainly

14/15. A mail hauberk might be worn underneath a padded garment or on top of it. Opinion was divided about the relative effectiveness.

BARDING

A covering for chargers generally made from cloth, though sometimes with connecting pieces of leather, horn or even mail at vulnerable points. A man-at-arms needed to have a 'barded' (or barbed) mount to qualify for his full rate of pay. The term 'covered' horses was also used to describe barding. A Scottish force in the 1290s had, as reported to Edward I by an English spy in the Scottish army, 'one hundred and fifty covered horses'.

included a variable number of hobelars. Lightly armoured and lightly mounted, the hobelars served as reconnaissance and foraging troops and were quite capable of imposing themselves on minor local resistance, but could not stand up to a body of men-at-arms and, in the event of a major battle, dismounted to serve among the infantry. It is a reasonable assumption that there were hobelars in Edward's army, but there is no evidence to suggest that they performed any significant role in the campaign as a whole or in the battle. That does not necessarily mean that they were present in smaller numbers than in previous campaigns, but merely that they did not register in surviving records or in chronicles. The former may simply be dependent on the fact that very little in the way of army records have survived and that since any hobelars served among the infantry on the battlefield there was nothing in the course of the engagement that distinguished them. On the other hand, one of Edward I's early campaigns had included a force of 200 mounted crossbowmen, who would undoubtedly be professional soldiers and possibly hired en bloc as a ready-formed distinct unit. No such unit appears in the pay and muster rolls – or horse valuations – of subsequent armies. It is not impossible that there were mounted crossbowmen in Edward II's 1314 army, but it would seem less than likely.

The mainstay of the mounted element of both armies was the man-at-arms, a term that covered every heavy cavalry man from the lowliest of the rank-and-file armoured horseman to the king himself.

It is understandable that many modern observers equate the medieval knight and the modern tank, though this really isn't a valid analogy. A force of tanks is seldom the mainstay and virtually never the sole constituent part of a major operational initiative, even if it does sometimes appear – superficially –

16. A re-enactor wearing the sort of brase and hose generally worn under clothing.

17. Closed helmets of this style were definitely old-fashioned by 1314, but were still serviceable and likely to have been passed on to the rank and file from better-equipped men-at-arms.

18. A selection of ordinary personal effects: a dagger, flint and steel, leather pouch, rosary and dice.

Bascinet

A close-fitting steel helmet with either an open face or a visor, the bascinet is generally assumed to have come into use in the mid-fourteenth century; however, there are several examples of bascinet being ordered and purchased from the 1290s onward. Given the duration of the war and the very fashion-conscious nature of the gentry and nobility on either side, it seems reasonable to assume that a great many of the man-at-arms class (and other men for whom soldiering was more than just an occasional venture when called upon to provide military service) had equipped themselves with bascinets before 1314.

Riveted Mail

Mail formed from a large number of small rings, generally rather less than 1cm across and with a gauge of metal of about 0.2mm. Riveted mail is distinguished by the fact that the two ends of each link have been flattened, placed over one another and then pierced and secured with a tiny rivet. The level of protection offered by riveted mail was not noticeably greater than that of butted mail, but the structural integrity was very much better.

to be the case. On the other hand, medieval operations were very frequently conducted exclusively by parties of men-at-arms. More medieval military records refer to the men-at-arms, or to 'knight service', than any other aspect of martial activity. Most 'knight service' was not discharged by men who were actual knights, or who even had any thought that they might become knights at some point; it was no more than a convenient administrative term to describe the nature of the service demanded rather than the men who discharged it.

The exact requirements of knight service, from the quality of horseflesh to the extent and quality of armour, changed significantly over the years from the twelfth to fifteenth centuries, but the term was always understood by both those who served and by those who paid their wages. The distinction between hobelars and men-at-arms did, however, become rather blurred; some years after Bannockburn, an English commander in Berwick made the reasonable point that it was hard to justify lower pay for his hobelars since they were as well armed (meaning 'armoured', in a medieval context) and as well mounted as the men-at-arms of the garrison. The man-at-arms of 1314 was very much the figure we might imagine as a 'knight in armour'. He wore a coat, gloves and hood of mail, a 'heater' shield, a light and incredibly strong sword about 3ft in length, a lance and a helmet. The closed barrel helm was fast giving way to the lighter bascinet style – so much so that by 1314 a barrel helm would probably have been seen as rather old-fashioned, since bascinets first start to appear in record evidence (purchase orders and receipts) nearly twenty years before Bannockburn. Most men-at-arms would have some plate armour, particularly to protect the arms, elbows and shoulders. These enhancements to the mail were often iron, but many wore pieces made from leather that had been boiled in wax, which provided a good level of protection for rather less weight and at a lower price.

The horse (charger) that the man-at-arms rode was not the sort of Clydesdale-sized beast of Victorian artworks, but was much more akin to a modern hunter. Strong, fast and remarkably nimble, chargers had to be very well-schooled and obedient creatures; the rider had to control his mount in battle with little use of the reins as he had to handle both his lance and his shield.

BUTTED MAIL

Easier, quicker and therefore very much cheaper
to produce than riveted mail, butted mail was
formed by simply bringing the two ends of each link
together and trusting to the circular nature of the
links to hold the shirt together.

Contrary to the romantic picture, the charger was not trained or encouraged to rear, bite or kick in battle, but to provide a secure platform for the rider to fight on. At the beginning of a campaign that was to be conducted outside of England (or periodically when in garrison service), each English man-at-arms had one of his horses valued by a committee appointed for the purpose. If the horse was lost on active service, he would be able to claim that value (or *restauro*) from the Crown, but in order to be eligible for his pay he needed to have a mount ready for battle every day. As such, virtually every man-at-arms ensured that he had a second mount (not subject to *restauro*) lest his primary charger was killed in action or became sick or lame. It seems unlikely that Scottish men-at-arms enjoyed this privilege, although it was not unknown for the Crown to provide a mount for individuals.

The men-at-arms provided the mobile striking force of the army, and might operate independently and at some distance from the main body. They might even, on occasion, form the entirety of a force: the Battle of Roslin was fought between two bodies of men-at-arms. However, they might serve on foot, not as a discrete body of men but rather as means of reinforcing the rank and file. It is possible that all the men-at-arms in King Robert's army served in that way, though there is a strong possibility that he kept a subtracted reserve of 500 men-at-arms to deal with any unexpected threat or opportunity. If he did not have such a force under command it would seem that at least a substantial proportion of the men-at-arms kept their horses sufficiently close at hand so that they could mount up to charge English archers and/or pursue Edward II after the battle.

Scottish and English men-at-arms were indistinguishable from one another and shared a common ethos and class; nevertheless, men certainly could make the transition from common soldier to man-at-arms or even to knight. They also shared a common advantage over the rank and file of either army. They were easily recognisable as men who, if captured, would almost certainly be able to raise a ransom.

Spearmen

The greatest number of troops on either side were spearmen. The bill had yet to become a staple close-combat weapon of

19. A man-at-arms and a spearman. The man-at-arms is wearing particularly extensive and heavy mail. By 1314 pieces of plate armour – particularly at the shoulder and elbow – were being added to supplement mail.

20. A chapel-de-fer or 'iron hat'. These were widely used throughout northern and western Europe in the thirteenth and fourteenth centuries.

21. It was possible, though a little difficult, to don mail unaided. Note the thickness of the padded garment under the mail.

22. A party of medieval spearmen would have looked rather like this, though the spears would have been a good deal longer.

English soldiers, and there were doubtless many varieties of pole-arm to be seen, but the majority of the close-combat infantry carried a stout spear, anything up to 50mm thick and 4m long.

As with the men-at-arms, there was no real difference in the equipment or appearance of Scottish and English spearmen. Some years after Bannockburn, Robert enacted legislation requiring all men with more than a specified level of wealth – lands worth £10 per annum or goods worth £40 per annum – to own a habergeon (which might mean either

23. A close-up of the same party of spearmen. Although individuals were responsible for the acquisition of their own equipment, there were well-understood minimum standards which had to be observed.

CUIR-BOUILLE

Formed by boiling pieces of leather in wax, *cuir-bouille* provided light, effective and relatively cheap protection. It was frequently used for shoulder, elbow or knee protection. Due to its organic nature, few examples have survived, but it was used extensively in the thirteenth and fourteenth centuries.

a padded jacket or possibly a short chain-mail shirt), a spear, a 'good iron' (generally taken to mean a helmet of some description) and a pair of armoured gloves. It is very likely that Robert's legislation was simply an attempt to confirm and codify the level of armament that was already expected, or even that it was a repetition of earlier legislation that has not survived. Re-affirming the legislation of previous kings was not unusual.

Poorer men were required to provide themselves with either a spear or a bow with arrows, but these men were seldom called upon to give service, save in cases of an extreme emergency such as an unexpected raid. Robert's stipulations should be seen as a minimum requirement rather than a general standard. The life of the individual soldier might well depend on the quality of his equipment and there was therefore an incentive to acquire the best protection one could afford; moreover, there had already been nearly two decades of near-continual warfare, so arms and armour were probably quite easy to come by and relatively cheap. Robert's forces had enjoyed several years of steady success so there was almost certainly quite a plentiful supply of material that had been captured on the battlefield or at the surrender of castles. The average English soldier had just as much to gain by ensuring that he would be as well protected in action as he could be and we should therefore expect that the overwhelming majority of common soldiers on either side were properly equipped for battle.

The only serious distinction between Scottish and English spearmen in 1314 lay in the quality and quantity of their experience and training. Men in both countries had an obligation to attend training days a couple of times every year, but Robert's army had been training intensively for several weeks. They had also developed a degree of confidence in their commanders and in one another through a succession of battlefield successes. The victories had been on a relatively small scale, but the cumulative effect was that the Scottish rank and file were ready for the fight. The fact that a considerable proportion of the men-at-arms were going to fight shoulder to shoulder with the common spearmen would have given them a greater confidence. If the gentry and nobility – and even the king himself – were prepared to dispense with their horses, then they were unmistakeably confident of victory.

Archers

The majority of modern accounts of Bannockburn explore – sometimes in some detail – the principal difference between England and Scottish archers; specifically that English archers used a longbow constructed from a piece of yew and Scottish archers used a short bow. The short bow, sometimes referred

24. An archer bending his bow. Although a skilled archer could hit a man at 300 yards, the arrow was unlikely to inflict serious damage on even a lightly armoured man.

25. A typical fourteenth-century archer.

to as the 'Ettrick' bow, has featured in many expositions of the battle for more than 100 years, but there is no trace of it in medieval records or narratives. There is no reason to assume that there was any difference at all between an English bow and a Scottish one, and we should be confident that if there had been a difference then at least one chronicler would have told us about it. In fact, the pay rolls and other material relating to both English and Scottish archers in the garrisons of Edward I, Edward II and Edward III make no distinction whatsoever between the two groups.

In 1314, the carefully drilled and well-organised bodies of archers that would be so critical to the outstanding longbow victories of Dupplin Muir, Crécy, Poitiers and Agincourt had yet to be developed. Archery was recognised as a potentially significant factor in breaking up formations of close-order spearmen so that the cavalry could make effective charges – as at Falkirk in 1298 – but the archers were still seen as a relatively minor ancillary to the main body of the infantry, let alone to the army as a whole. Even in the most spectacular longbow victories of later years, the outcome of the battle still had to be secured with hard combat between the spearmen and men-at-arms on either side.

The traditional view of medieval war throughout Europe presents a picture of two quite separate bodies of men in the same army: one group consisting of heavily armoured knights and the other of impoverished and bedraggled foot soldiers whose chief function was to be killed by their social and political superiors. The picture starts to break down when English archers are brought into the equation, but is still an element in the 'perceived history' of the Middle Ages.

Some loose assumptions about the nature of the English army in particular have encouraged the belief that the infantry were little more than a mob of men with spears. These assumptions are based chiefly on a widespread belief that only archers and men-at-arms were of any significance in battle, the rate of pay on offer and the number of English soldiers granted pardons in exchange for service. For the latter, it is far too simplistic to assume that a man accused of a criminal offence would necessarily be poor. In fact, one could argue that his criminality might well have made him rather better off than most people. The rate of pay –

customarily in the region of 2*d* per day – was certainly small and did not compare well with agricultural day labour, let alone with skilled employment of any kind, but it is more valid to see that sum as an allowance for expenses rather than a wage.

Much the same applies to the shilling (12*d*) per day paid to men-at-arms or the 2 shillings paid to knights. The distinction in rate was not, however, a reflection of greater financial burdens, but rather an acknowledgement of the social superiority of knighthood. Undoubtedly some men managed to serve with less (or poorer quality) equipment than they should have had and still successfully drew their pay, but on the whole, we should see both armies as consisting of properly equipped men bearing the arms and armour that the law required them to keep, whether there was war or peace. However, even the higher rate of pay for knights was probably insufficient to cover the outlay costs involved, let alone the time that had to be devoted to training.

The Tactics

A great deal of comment about the nature of medieval armies and their deployment for battle is still heavily influenced by what Victorian antiquarians wanted to think and by questionable deductions from disparate source materials which are not always – if at all – relevant.

Two particularly important factors have led to widely held misapprehensions. Oman and Gardiner both took the view that the Scots had fought a defensive battle. Quite why they thought this is not clear, since both had evidently read the narrative sources. The most probable answer is that they simply assumed that infantry could never attack an opponent with a stronger cavalry element, especially if it included a powerful force of heavily armoured knights and men-at-arms.

SURCOAT

A form of cloth overall, the surcoat helped to protect the bearer – generally a member of the gentry or nobility – from the elements, and was a means of showing his coat of arms. Other than those of a few prominent individuals, the coat of arms itself was often rather meaningless since there were many thousands of them, but it did indicate the social and economic class of the bearer and therefore whether or not he would be worth a ransom if captured.

26. Very few soldiers would have had the luxury of a sophisticated tent like this one.

SCHILTROMS

Generally perceived as huge circular bodies of men with spears facing outward as a protection against cavalry, there is, however, only one known example of a Scottish army deploying as a group of circular schiltroms: Falkirk in 1298. In practice, the term simply means a body of close-order spearmen of any shape, but almost always a rectangular arrangement.

They may also have been misled in their assumptions about the main battle by the fact that on the first day Robert's formation took a defensive stance, but it did so in a position which invited an attack and was therefore essentially a hostile posture; Robert was looking for a fight, not trying to dissuade his enemy. Similarly, Moray's force, though it stood to receive a charge, had, again, invited that attack by barring the route to Stirling. In fact, Moray had deliberately moved to a position that, superficially at least, would favour a cavalry action.

Popular perceptions and assumptions about the Scots fighting a defensive battle have also been reinforced by observations about other battles – most notably Falkirk, where Wallace's army stood still against Edward I and was roundly defeated. Because Wallace's army was deployed in four large circular formations, there has been a tendency to believe that this was the traditional and customary battlefield posture of medieval Scottish armies. In reality, so far as we know, Falkirk was the one and only occasion where this approach was used, and it was chosen from a lack of other choices. Edward I had stolen a march on Wallace and he could see no other practical option. In short, he had a plan for avoiding defeat – which did not work – but no plan for victory. Apart from Falkirk, there is only one example of a Scottish infantry force of any size,

27. With their spear points presented to the enemy in a thick hedge, a schiltrom was virtually invulnerable to cavalry attacks.

let alone a whole army, deploying in a circular or near-circular formation: Moray's action on the first day of Bannockburn.

The term 'schiltron' or 'schiltrom' has become associated with these round spear formations – though for medieval writers the term did not imply any particular shape, simply a dense body of infantry – and it has become customary to assume that Robert's army deployed in circular formations. This despite the fact that the source material clearly tells us that on the day of the main action the Scots marched down from the high ground through woods and then formed a moving wall of infantry stretching from the Pelstream to the Bannock.

Clearly – even if various writers have thought otherwise – moving a body of 1,500 or more men in a vast circle would be extremely difficult to achieve on a parade ground with highly trained professional soldiers and modern systems of foot-drill and articulation, but in the Middle Ages such systems did not exist. In fact, the 'cadenced' marching (that is to say moving the legs in strict time 'left, right, left, right, left, right'), which is the basis of all precision foot-drill and that we take for granted when we see a troops on parade, would not be invented for another 300 years or more. Medieval armies – and for that matter classical armies before them and early modern armies after – moved in column and fought in line as far as possible. Bringing his troops down the slope in column and then turning the head of each column to the left or right, halting them and then turning the entire column to face the enemy, thus forming the line of battle, would have been infinitely more practical than trying to manoeuvre a tightly packed 'hedgehog' formation.

Medieval battle is often depicted as a massive free-for-all of hundreds or even thousands of individual combats milling about the battlefield. In reality, effective combat was a matter of bringing formations together into battle at a single blow. This was true for both infantry and cavalry. The impact of a mounted charge was very much reduced if the leading ranks arrived in a piecemeal fashion.

The free-for-all view is undermined by the nature of the weapons themselves. Although most, if not all, men carried a sword, axe or mace, for most soldiers the primary weapon in battle – as opposed to single combats – was the spear or lance. In individual combat, a man with a sword or axe might be able to slip past the spear point of his adversary and would then have a significant advantage. In a battle, the man with a sword would have to evade or beat away not just one spear point, but perhaps a dozen or more before he could get close enough to land a blow with his axe or mace. To take an example from nature, a hedgehog is well protected by having a great array of spines, but would be extremely vulnerable to attack if it had only one spine, however sharp and strong that spine might be. The spear and the lance were only at their most effective if they were used in large numbers operating in close co-operation. This could only be achieved by working hard to maintain a uniform formation in close order and by ensuring that as many men as possible were in a position to inflict blows on the enemy. For this reason, medieval close-combat troops almost invariably moved into battle in linear bodies. The formation had to be several ranks deep in order to continue to present an array of spear points to the enemy, so the 'dressing' of the unit – the matter of maintaining regular ranks and files – was of paramount importance.

Keeping to a regular formation also had the added benefit of ensuring that men knew who they were fighting. Quite simply, the linear formations meant that the soldier was aware that the enemy were the men facing him and that his comrades were those facing in the same direction as himself. This could not possibly be achieved if the action degenerated into a great number of individuals fighting other individuals, and in an age before uniforms or other forms of battlefield identification, this was a crucial matter. Traditionally, heraldry has been seen as

SHIELD

Every man-at-arms, and most other soldiers, would have a shield in his personal arsenal; it had a vital function in mounted and dismounted combat. Made from plywood, the shield had to be thick enough to offer decent protection against arrows, swords, spears and axes, and was in fact the first 'line of defence' for the soldier. It is extremely difficult to handle a long spear effectively while carrying a shield and it is therefore very likely that the rank-and-file Scottish infantry dispensed with their shields at Bannockburn; they do not figure in the descriptions of Scottish troops in contemporary material relating to the battle, but would have been invaluable in other circumstances.

an important factor in identifying friend from foe, but this was simply not the case. Heraldic colours and symbols were limited in number, but there were still many thousands of possible permutations. Although efforts were made – and occasionally court cases pursued – to prevent duplication, there might be very little difference between one coat of arms and another. Even if an individual could memorise thousands of different shields, and who bore them and which side they were on, it could prove very difficult to identify them accurately in the heat of battle.

This does not mean that heraldic devices were without value. A lot of men would have been aware of a few specific examples. In the case of King Robert or King Edward, that recognition would be virtually universal, and many people would recognise the arms of a handful of great lords or particularly famous warriors like de Valence, Carrick, Douglas or Clifford. The banners of these men would be prominently displayed, perhaps beside a national or royal ensign, and would be a means of identification; even so, the direction of approach and the close proximity of one's comrades would have been much more significant once battle was joined.

The tactical roles of the various troop types were not complicated: spears, bows, cavalry all needed to act together efficiently to procure victory. Archers were very vulnerable if not supported by close-combat troops, and close-combat troops could be equally vulnerable to archery if they had no archer support. The infantry were not an afterthought in medieval armies; in fact, they would generally constitute at least 70 per cent of the army and often as much as 90 per cent. In 1314, Edward specifically called for a good turnout of foot soldiers since he anticipated operations in territory where the cavalry would not be able to operate effectively.

Heavy cavalry could be devastating in the right circumstances, but – as the engagements at Bannockburn would demonstrate all too clearly – were virtually powerless against steady and determined infantry. The common-espoused view that men-at-arms could simple crash through infantry is not borne out by the experience of medieval battle. Although it is possible to

28. Articulated armour for the legs and arms was becoming increasingly common by 1314. This re-enactor is mounted on a 'covered' or 'barded' horse, though in the fourteenth century the barding would have consisted of several layers of cloth to reduce the effectiveness of arrows and edged weapons.

persuade a man to throw himself into the fight against a hedge of spear points, the average horse is a sensible creature and will simply slow to a halt before it makes contact. To some degree, the reluctance of the horse can be overcome by training, but not, as a rule, to the point of the horse galloping full tilt on to the spears. Combat between mounted men-at-arms was a rather different matter. Opposing bodies of cavalry did not present anything like the same close-set array of threatening implements as a body of infantry; even so, in order to keep the formation as tight as possible, it seems probable that most cavalry clashes were conducted at a round trot rather than a flat-out gallop. Discipline in the charge was certainly seen as an important, even crucial, factor. Men who had a knight-service commitment almost invariably had an obligation to take part in the hunting activities of their superior. Obviously this was a social activity, but it had a military aspect in that the members of the hunt became accustomed to riding in close proximity, riding over difficult terrain and generally acting as a team under one leader. Keeping control of the charge was a serious business. There are several examples of men being disciplined – usually with a fine – for advancing 'ahead of the king's banner'. This does not imply that the king was actually present, but rather that a royal or national ensign was carried in the front rank of the formation and that riding on ahead of it could disrupt the integrity and thus the effectiveness of the formation. Overall, medieval armies were much more carefully organised than traditional depictions would suggest, and we should bear that in mind when we consider the process of individual battles.

BEFORE
THE BATTLE

Edward II's Forces

Edward started the process of raising an army as early as October 1313 and was probably already planning an expedition before that. Doubtless he would have mounted a major response to Robert earlier had it not been for his internal political difficulties, his problems in France – not least the thorny business of negotiating the performance of the homage that he owed for Gascony – and the great burden of debt that he had inherited from his father. Similarly, Robert had started gathering his troops several weeks before the campaign and was able to have his forces in place before the English army mustered at Berwick and Wark.

The size of the Bannockburn armies has been the subject of much debate. Chronicle figures simply cannot be taken at face value. Barbour's claim that there were 30,000 Scots and 100,000 English has been the basis for many estimates, though largely this would seem to be a matter of later writers assuming that he had inflated the armies by a factor of four, resulting in 7,500 Scots and 25,000 English. These figures are not altogether impossible, but in fact Barbour was not really offering figures to be taken literally. Many medieval authors used multiples of three to give an idea of scale in much the same way that we might use the term 'thousands' or even 'millions' when we just mean 'a lot'. In medieval literature 300 can mean 'a modest body', 3,000 can be taken to indicate 'a substantial body' and 30,000 to mean 'a very large body'. Barbour's use of '30,000' for the Scots and '100,000' for the English is probably best interpreted as meaning that the Scottish army was very large and the English army was very much larger still. For Barbour, and his audience,

29. Grave effigy of Sir Roger de Trumpington. This image dates from about 1280; by the time of Bannockburn the absence of any plate armour other than knee protection would have made the bearer look rather outdated, but would still have been acceptable as equipment for a man-at-arms.

the key information was that King Robert had assembled a massive force from across the country, demonstrating his political power. That said, Barbour did not shy away from the fact that there were still Scots in the English camp, telling us that Edward had the services of a great company of Scottish men-at-arms from Lothian. Although this is undoubtedly true, the claim does require a little examination. It is probably reasonable to assume that the company in question was drawn from more than just Lothian.

Although Roxburgh had fallen to the Bruce party in February 1314 and Edinburgh only a month later, It is more than likely that Robert had not, as yet, been able to fully assert his power in Roxburghshire and Lothian; even if he had, there would almost inevitably be men who felt that Edward would be able to crush Robert in the event of a major battle and that even if there was no actual engagement, he would be able to recover and repair the castles and re-impose his government, at least in southern Scotland. For men in that position, turning out for the Bruce party would have been an enormous risk no matter if they were supportive of Robert's kingship. If Edward was able to restore his authority, they would face the strong possibility of forfeiture or, if captured, the death penalty for treason.

Not all Scots were happy about Robert's acquisition of the throne in the first place; he was, after all, a usurper. Furthermore, there was no strong tradition of political leadership by the Bruce family in the south-east of Scotland. So long as King John's heir was alive, Robert could not be the legitimate king. Additionally, some of those who might have been willing to accept his kingship would have been discouraged by the fact that he had killed a political rival in a church and had been excommunicated.

Although there was clearly still opposition to Robert's reign and, naturally, doubts that he could withstand Edward's invasion, the numbers in Barbour's 'great company' were hardly enough to make a major contribution to Edward's army. Even under the best of circumstances, it is unlikely that Lothian, Berwickshire and Roxburghshire combined could raise more than a few hundred men-at-arms, and there is nothing to indicate that Edward II – or his father for that matter – ever made any effort to raise infantry service from these counties. The summer of 1314 was not, in any case, the best of circumstances. Although Robert could not be confident of exerting his authority to the utmost degree in the south-east, he certainly had more sway there than Edward II, so it is unlikely that the contribution of Lothian men-at-arms amounted to more than a few score, especially given that a party who did attempt to join the English army arrived in the vicinity only to discover that Edward had already been defeated and therefore promptly changed sides.

These Lothian men were not, however, the only Scots in Edward's allegiance. A considerable number of Scots who had not come into King Robert's peace were living as pensioners of the English Crown. Some had lost their lands because they had refused to renounce their allegiance to the Comyn family or to King John or to King Edward; others had been refused admission to the Bruce party because of acts in the past. For these men, the only hope of recovering their lands and titles was through service to the Plantagenet cause. They were relatively few in number, but their presence did have a political significance, since it was an indication that there was some Scottish support for Edward's rule, but, like the company of Lothian men, their contribution to the man-at-arms element of Edward's army was marginal.

Although we do not have accurate information about the size of Edward's army, we can make some viable deductions based on what we know of previous and later expeditions for which the pay rolls and other record material survive. This was a particularly large force by the standards of late English medieval armies, but it was nothing like the 100,000 men suggested by Barbour. The major armies recruited for service in Scotland under Edward I and Edward II included a heavy cavalry element of about 2,500 men-at-arms, as shown by horse valuations and pay rolls. This is a little misleading since various categories of men did not have their service recorded. A few chose not to serve for pay and a rather large number served without pay to gain pardons for crimes, but neither category amounted to a very significant portion of the cavalry element. There would have been similar elements in the army of 1314, but there were also a number of major lords – the Earl of Lancaster, for example – who refused to serve at all. On balance, the figure of 2,500 men-at-arms is probably a valid assessment. In other armies of a similar scale in this period, the men-at-arms were divided into four units, three led by important nobles and one, rather larger than the others, nominally directly under the king's command. Assuming that the 1314 army adhered to this structure then three bodies of about 500 men and one of 1,000 would fit the evidence rather well.

The situation is less clear in regard to the infantry. Edward issued writs to raise over 21,000 men, but it is clear from other armies of the period that actual recruitment seldom exceeded two-thirds of what was called for. Additionally, desertion was a constant problem, though the 1314 army was probably not in existence for long enough for that to have become a critical factor. Conscription was not the sole source of men: there would have been additional troops who served to procure pardons and some who volunteered in search of plunder or adventure or to avoid troubles at home, but these are unlikely to have constituted a very significant number. In total, it is unlikely that Edward had much more than 15,000 infantry under his command by the time the army made camp at Stirling on 23 June, and probably something closer to 12,000 would be a more realistic estimate. However, naturally, there would have been a substantial number of non-combatants as well.

Of these 12–15,000 infantry, the greater number would certainly have been spearmen, the balance being archers, but we should not assume that the latter were the equivalent of the well-drilled bowmen of the English armies of Edward II's reign. It seems very likely that a random proportion were simply issued with bows at the time of enlistment or at the muster, regardless of ability. This is probably less significant than it might at first seem. Obviously, it would result in there being only a very small number of skilled marksmen, but the chief function of the archers would be to shoot at large, closely packed formations of spearmen or cavalry – hardly the most demanding of targets.

Like the cavalry, the infantry were not simply an amorphous horde of troops. There was a system of articulation. We cannot be absolutely certain that the army of 1314 utilised the same system as those of the preceding and subsequent decades, but it would be anomalous if it did not – so much so that we should expect that some comment would have survived. The evidence from other English armies indicates three clear levels of administrative articulation: large units commanded by officers called 'millenars', which consisted of smaller units commanded by 'centenars', which in turn were made up of smaller units under the command of 'vintenars'. It would be simplistic to assume that these units were necessarily exactly 1,000 or 100 or 20 strong respectively, but there is a clear implication that they would have been of that order. We know from record material that there were men who were referred to as 'corporals' and 'petty officers', but it is not clear whether these were any more than alternative terms for the lowest rank of infantry leaders, the vintenars. There is a possibility that when an army was newly mustered, these three levels of articulation did actually reflect numerical strength quite accurately, though clearly desertion, sickness and, of course, combat would all have an effect – especially desertion, which was clearly a perennial problem for English armies operating in Scotland to a far larger degree than in those deployed to France or Ireland, simply because it was a much more practical proposition for an individual or a group of men to return home on foot or horse. For operational purposes, it seems likely that the commands of the millenars were combined into large units.

Barbour's assertion that the English army was in ten divisions is probably better seen as literary rather than literal, though it is possible that he had access to material that he did not necessarily fully understand, and that the English army really was organised in ten divisions of infantry in the form of the commands of the millenars. To what extent these units were tactical entities as well as administrative ones is impossible to say, yet there is at least one example of a millenar being held responsible for the failure of the men of his formation to provide an adequate night guard on campaign.

Edward's infantry was not a mere afterthought. He and his subordinates were familiar with fighting in Scotland and Edward was eager to ensure that a large infantry force was raised, since he believed that there might well be extensive fighting in difficult countryside, where the cavalry could not operate effectively.

Robert I's Forces

The Scottish army was certainly rather smaller than that of Edward II, which is no more than we should expect given the disparity in population. We can, however, be reasonably confident that Robert did not raise an army based simply on numbers. The tactics he adopted depended on having well-equipped infantry and we are told by Barbour that in the weeks before the battle Robert turned away volunteers who did not have adequate armour and weapons.

It is much harder to identify any form of articulation in the Scottish army, though clearly there must have been one to enable administration of a force of several thousand men, if only for the purposes of regulating working parties and issuing rations. Since it is clear that Robert concentrated his troops at Stirling some weeks before the battle it is reasonable to assume that there was some form of articulation at various levels to facilitate personal and unit training. It is possible to discern an element of this in the leadership structure. The Earl of Moray had command of a major portion of the army – a body of 2,000 men or more – but in his action near St Ninian's chapel on the first day of the battle, he took only a portion of that force into the fight. Barbour describes Moray's force in that engagement as being 500 men 'of his own leding' (leading). This implies that they were men who owed him their military service directly in his capacity as Earl of Moray. This highlights a difference in the political structures of England and Scotland. After the conquest of 1066, William the Conqueror granted the title of 'earl' of this or that county to his more prominent followers, but the title was not directly attached to the land; it was, essentially, honorific.

In Scotland – as in France or pre-conquest England – an earl was a regional potentate with a wide variety of powers, including the administration of certain aspects of justice and responsibility for raising troops on behalf of the king. Scotland did not consist of earldoms alone, and, as in England, the sheriff or the burgh council had an obligation to raise a certain number of men when required. The earl's

30. Looking south from the approximate position of King Robert's division on the afternoon of 23 June.

official responsibility might – in fact, perhaps generally did – extend beyond his own lands within the earldom, but even if certain landholders were exempted from his authority, they could hardly afford to ignore the most powerful man in the area. It was a system that could be open to abuse. When King Robert was Earl of Carrick, he was obliged to promise not to use his position as an earl to demand military service for his own purposes from men who were not his tenants but happened to reside within the bounds of his authority, but only to call them out in the national interest.

The king and the greater lords, such as the Earls of Carrick or Moray, had two quite separate forms of military responsibility.

31. The contemporary material indicates that the Scots moved down to the plain from higher ground in the New Park. They probably formed up in the area where the new Bannockburn High School stands.

32. Once the Scots had formed up they had to negotiate this steep slope before deploying on the plain.

Mustering the rank and file of the army was a matter of administering the 'common army' service which was, in theory, due from every able-bodied man, but in practice was generally only demanded from men of a certain level of wealth – those who could afford to purchase the necessary equipment. The other was knight service: a military obligation on those who held estates – usually heritably – in exchange for service as men-at-arms, regardless of whether they were knights. A large estate might be held in exchange for the service of five or ten knights or more and a small one might be held for a fraction of the service of a knight. How exactly fractional service was discharged is not clear from the record evidence, and some of

33. A Scottish 'birlinn' or galley. Vessels like this were used extensively by Robert I in his campaigns on the west coast of Scotland. A number of barons and other landholders were obliged to provide manned warships like this for their 'knight service' rather than serving as mounted men-at-arms, though it was not uncommon for such men to serve in both capacities as required.

EARLDOM

In England the title of 'earl' was a heritable honour, but it did not carry any specific legal or administrative responsibility. The Earl of Gloucester or the Earl of Cornwall did not have any particular rights, privileges or duties within those counties, but any earl was likely to hold a great deal of property spread across the whole country and be an important figure in the national political community accordingly. This was not the case in other European kingdoms. In France or Scotland an earl would wield a great deal of almost sub-regal power – holding courts, administering local defence, raising troops for national armies – but only within his stated jurisdiction. The earl did not, however, own all the land in his county. Major properties within the earldom might be held by any number of people and might in some instances be excused various obligations to the local earl.

it may have been delivered in the form of archer service or a monetary payment, or as a shared expense between a number of neighbours who each owed a fraction of a knight to the king's army. The latter was probably more prevalent than one might expect, since a good deal of fractional knight service came about through the division of a property between female heirs, and the two or more properties that came into being by that route would, as a rule, be adjacent to one another.

The body of men-at-arms raised from knight service was small compared with that available to the King of England, but was not insubstantial. Although Robert did not as yet have absolute control in some of the areas that would traditionally have produced the greatest numbers of men-at-arms, it is most likely that nearly two decades of war – and several years of steady military success – would have produced a number of men who would not normally have aspired to knight service, but for whom war presented an opportunity for social advancement. On balance, it would not be remarkable if Robert had something in the region of 1,000 men-at-arms under his command in June 1314.

Another possible aspect of articulation is archery. There are a number of references from both later and earlier sources that refer to an individual being the leader of Scottish archers. It is possible, therefore, that there was a capacity for, or perhaps even general practice of, organising the archers as one or more separate commands within the army structure. Given the relatively small numbers involved – perhaps 10 per cent of the entire strength – this would make sense both administratively and tactically, but the evidence is far too meagre to come to any firm conclusions. On balance, given the sum of what we know of the strength and nature of Scottish and English armies of the later medieval period, we might make an informed guess that the armies of 1314 are unlikely to have exceeded 7–8,000 Scots and 16–18,000 English at most.

The English army is unlikely to have been any smaller than 10,000 foot and 2,000 men-at-arms, but is equally unlikely to have been any greater than 16,000 foot and 3,000 men-at-arms. The Scottish army almost certainly falls with the range of 5,000 foot and 1,000 men-at-arms (though many, and perhaps all, certainly served on foot in the main engagement), with an upper limit of perhaps 8,000 infantry.

These are, however, estimates of combat strength; they take no account of the large numbers of ancillary staff that undoubtedly accompanied both armies and we cannot be totally certain that records of all the contributions to the army have survived. Edward certainly called for troops from Ireland, but there is no clear evidence to indicate that they were ever actually raised, let alone that they made the journey to Scotland or, if they did, that they joined the main army before the battle. However, it would seem much more probable than not that if they had crossed over to Scotland there would be some record of their passage, their activity or their return (or failure to return) to Ireland.

THE BATTLEFIELD

The First Day

Stirling was hardly *terra incognita* to Edward in 1314. He had very probably been there himself during the time he had spent in Scotland, and if he had not visited there himself, at least some of his senior officers – particularly those who had held offices in the occupation government – had done so in the past. The English army left its mustering areas at Wark and Berwick on 17 or 18 June and marched on Edinburgh through Lauderdale and Tweeddale. Since Edinburgh castle had fallen to the Scots three months previously, there was little reason to go to Edinburgh other than possibly to meet up with a convoy of supply shipping and to intimate to the local populace that the occupation government was being resurrected. The army marched westward to Falkirk, where it spent the night of 22/23 June before moving on toward Stirling. They had made reasonably good time, but it was clearly far from being a forced march – presumably a deliberate policy to ensure that the army was not unduly tired when it arrived in what Edward and his lieutenants hoped would be the battle area. However, they believed – not unreasonably – that Robert might well try to avoid a general engagement.

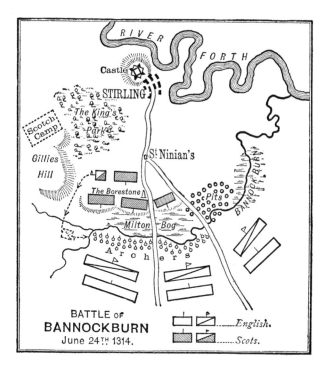

34. *The Battle of Bannockburn as envisaged by Oman and Gardiner, though it bears very little resemblance to the contemporary source material.*

At some point during the march, two formations were detached from the main body of the army, a force under the Earls of Gloucester and Hereford taking what we might consider the main road from Falkirk straight to Stirling and a second force consisting entirely of men-at-arms under Sir Robert de Clifford and Sir Henry de Beaumont – including Sir Thomas Grey, father of the author of *Scalacronica* – moving closer to the course of the River Forth on the low ground to the east of the New Park.

These operations were undertaken for a variety of purposes. One role of the cavalry force under Clifford and Beaumont was clearly to bring about a technical relief of the garrison in Stirling castle. In a sense, this was almost superfluous given that the English army had arrived within striking distance and in great force within the stipulated period, but protocol and form were important aspects of medieval war and politics. Bringing a force into the castle would certainly satisfy the requirements of the surrender compact, but it would also conform to the spirit of the age. It would be a feat of arms – an act of chivalry – and would play well in chronicle accounts, which Edward could be confident would be written after the

35. The open farmland on which he main battle took place. Contrary to Victorian interpretations, all of the contemporary material makes it clear than the main engagement took place on firm ground, not among bogs and marshes.

campaign; in fact, he had brought along the noted English poet Friar Baston for that very purpose.

There were more practical considerations. Edward was determined to bring the Scots to battle and was concerned – understandably, given the extensive experience of his own and his father's Scottish campaigns – that King Robert would not stand and fight, but would withdraw into the west or north and avoid a major engagement until such time as a shortage of food and money forced Edward to abandon the campaign.

Placing a strong mobile force to the eastern flank and rear of the enemy might not prevent the Scots from retreating, but it would certainly make the process more difficult, since a largely infantry army on the march would be vulnerable to sudden cavalry attacks. Alternatively, if the Scots did not withdraw, Edward and his subordinates would hope to gather intelligence about their strength and dispositions. The other force, under Gloucester and Hereford, had a similar role. The Scots could hardly ignore their presence and must either try to block their path to Stirling or take to their heels and therefore allow the English a clear passage to the town. That would not have been the preferred option for Edward as he was anxious to inflict a serious defeat on the Scots, but it would not be completely unattractive. Robert had brought a large force to Stirling and kept them there for weeks of training. If he did not put his army to any use, his prestige as a military leader would be undermined, and his political credibility as the man best suited for protecting Scotland from invasion would be severely compromised. Robert had raised large forces in the past and avoided battle, but he could not do so indefinitely without impairing his reputation and authority.

With any luck, from Edward's perspective, the two forces would achieve one or more of a number of positive outcomes. The castle would be relieved and there might be one or more actions in which his forces would be successful, possibly forcing Robert to abandon the area entirely. It was even possible that one successful fight, even on a relatively small scale, might demoralise the Scots so much that their army might disintegrate; this had, after all, been the case at Dunbar in 1296. Although these were all acceptable possibilities, the real hope was that the two forces would not only reveal everything about the strength and position of the Scots, but that they would effectively pin the enemy and force Robert to give battle whether he wanted to or not.

Edward could afford to be quite confident about the enterprise. The smaller cavalry force moving between the Scottish positions to their left and the River Forth on their right

36. The Bannock burn. The burn was probably rather wider in 1314, but even today it has a very soft and muddy floor which would be a considerable barrier to armoured men trying to escape the battlefield.

was powerful enough to take on fairly substantial opposition and mobile enough to avoid a major body of the enemy if that became necessary. The large force under Hereford and Gloucester might well score a significant victory by itself, but if the enemy proved to be too strong for them, it would provide a barrier to the Scots so that the rest of Edward's army could complete their march to a suitable campsite.

The only suitable site for such a large force lay between the Pelstream and the Bannock burns. Although Edward and, to a lesser degree, his subordinates have been the subject of a great deal of criticism for their choice of a camp, they really had very limited options. Like any medieval army, Edward's force included a very large number of horses and a considerable quantity of oxen as draught animals and as beef on the hoof, in addition to perhaps 15,000 men or more. All of these would require fresh water in large amounts and the two streams – each rather larger then than they are today due to drainage developments that have changed the water course considerably – would be absolutely vital if the army and the animals were not to suffer dehydration at the end of a day's march in hot, sunny weather. The strip between the burns was more than large enough to accommodate the army and its baggage, but the burns themselves would give a degree of protection against any Scottish surprise attacks during the short summer nights. This was considered – by Edward at least – to be a real possibility. The campsite would not provide any sort of barrier between the English army and the Scots, who were camped on the higher ground to the west, but neither Edward nor his lieutenants seems to have been at all concerned that the Scots might mount a direct full-scale attack from the high ground. Given their lengthy experience of fighting in Scotland, this was not an unreasonable conclusion; to date, the challenge had been more a matter of getting the Scots to commit to battle at

---

CARSE

A carse is a low-lying area which is prone to flooding,
or at least saturation, during the winter months, but
forms dry pasture in the spring and summer.

---

all, let alone to make a set-piece attack on firm, open ground
that would favour greater numerical strength in general and
especially the far larger contingent of heavy cavalry available
to Edward.

The Scots, of course, were waiting for the arrival of Edward's
army. The three main formations of the army, commanded
by the king, the Earl of Carrick and the Earl of Moray, were
all stationed on the high ground of the New Park, with the
baggage and stores to the rear, possibly around the area of the
southern end of the King's Park. The King's Division was closest
to the enemy, with Carrick's men to the rear and Moray's troops
further to the north, where they could intervene if an English
force marched across the farmland to the east of the king's
position. Carrick, roughly midway between the two, could
march quickly to the aid of either the king or Moray if necessary,
but could remain out of sight until required.

Gloucester and Hereford's force marched well in advance
of the main body of the army and crossed the stretch of the
Bannock burn, which lies to the south of the present National
Trust for Scotland Visitor Centre, and proceeded up the slope
toward the nearest Scottish position.

Gloucester and Hereford may have thought that they
were facing the entire Scottish army, which they must have
known would have been a rather larger force than their own,
but more realistically they were probably aware that they
would be encountering only a portion of King Robert's force.

37. A view toward 'The Entry', where the Earls of Gloucester and Hereford made the first attack and where de Bohun was killed in a single combat with King Robert.

Assuming that they were aware of de Bohun's unsuccessful attack on King Robert, they would very likely have deduced that the enemy to their front would consist of Robert's own immediate command and that there was therefore probably not a great discrepancy in numbers, but even if they did not, they would have been well aware that over the preceding decade and more since Falkirk, the Scots had not often chosen to make a stand in front of a determined advance. In that light, it was not an unreasonable decision to make an attempt to dislodge the Scots from their position and even possibly cause them to panic and desert the battlefield in disorder.

The Scottish position was, however, naturally strong and may have been enhanced to favour a defensive stand. At the top of the rise, the road passed into an area known as 'The Entry', where the gap between two stretches of woodland became narrower to the left and right of the road. The governor of Stirling castle had sent a report to Edward informing him that the Scots had been mustering at the New Park, training and busily blocking the paths in the woodland – presumably to prevent bodies of troops from outflanking their position. According to some sources, the Scots had also dug narrow pits or 'pots' at a particular location and had camouflaged these with sticks and grass so that unwary horsemen might ride into them and be thrown when their horses stepped into them and broke their legs. It seems most likely that this was the location of the 'pots', though no sign of them has ever emerged from aerial photography or archaeological surveys.

The purpose of such a stratagem was not so much to inflict casualties as to deny sections of the terrain to the enemy. As soon as the first rider fell from his horse, his comrades would be aware of the danger and act accordingly. Assuming that the pots were distributed on either side of the road, they would have the effect of denying a flank approach against the Scots and of funnelling the English advance toward Scottish spears and at the same time giving protection to the Scottish archers among the trees on either side. Regardless of the existence or otherwise of the pots, the English force moved into The Entry, presumably hoping to force their way along the road to Stirling, but found their route blocked by a large body of spearmen and Scottish archers who shot at them from woods on either flank.

There was an action, but it does not seem to have lasted for very long; Gloucester and Hereford could make no headway and there was little point in standing around taking casualties if they could not make progress toward Stirling castle, so they broke off the action and made their way back down the slope and then eastwards to the camp area. There is no reason to assume that Gloucester and Hereford's force had been weakened in any material way either in confidence or numbers, but the action had been beneficial to the Scots. It did not prove that cavalry without adequate infantry support were at a disadvantage when confronted by steady infantry – that had been demonstrated many times in the past – but it was certainly a boost to Scottish morale, which was already high after King Robert's rather public dispatch of Sir Henry de Bohun in a single combat.

There was a wider consideration, however. Edward's army had suffered a reverse, and Robert could now, if he chose, withdraw and avoid a major battle without damaging his political standing in the community. Part of the price of gathering a large army was that if he never brought the troops into action he would eventually start to look indecisive, even weak, which – particularly as a usurper – he could not afford if he was to retain the credibility and prestige necessary for effective kingship.

No sooner was this engagement over, than Robert received news of another development. While Gloucester and Hereford had been approaching along the main road, the second force of men-at-arms under the command of Clifford and Beaumont had been moving along another road through the fields to the east of the New Park and were headed toward the area around St Ninian's chapel, presumably en route to relieve the Stirling castle garrison and thus fulfil the bargain struck between the commander, Sir Philip Moubray, and the Earl of Carrick some three months earlier. Formally discharging the pact was of limited significance; in fact, it had possibly already been dealt with since, according to Barbour, the agreement was that an English army had to come within 3 leagues of the castle for a relief to be recognised. The term 'league' is a challenging one and often appears in chronicles without absolute clarity as to whether it means 1 mile or 3, but assuming that in this context the term meant 3 miles, the castle had already been relieved by the afternoon of 23 June, and Moubray was therefore no longer bound to surrender his post. More realistically, the

38. A well-equipped infantry man of the fourteenth century, with a chapel-de-fer helmet and two thin, padded garments, one under his mail and another over it.

security or otherwise of the garrison would depend on the developments of the next twenty-four hours or so. If the Scots withdrew, the castle would be safe for as long as a major

English army could be maintained in Scotland. If Edward retired to England without striking a major blow against the Bruce administration and imposing his own government securely in its place, the Scots would simply return and lay a new siege. Equally, if Edward was able to bring Robert to battle and defeat him, the Bruce cause would probably be fatally compromised, even if Robert was able to escape with his life. In all likelihood, no one on the English side – and very few among the Scots – had really given much thought to the possibility that Robert might actually force a battle, let alone that he might win it decisively.

Even so, honour rather demanded that an effort be made to relieve the castle and there was the additional potential value of gaining better information about the strength, dispositions and intentions of the Scottish army.

It seemed to King Robert that the Earl of Moray had lost concentration and that Beaumont and Clifford would be able to reach Stirling unmolested unless immediate action was taken. He told Moray that a 'Rose was fallen from his Chaplet' (Barbour) – that he had blotted his copybook – and sent him off to deal with the situation. Moray was the commander of a major formation within the army, probably about one-quarter of the total strength and about one-third of the main strength of the Scots, the rank-and-file spearmen, but he chose to take only a portion of that strength into the fight. Instead he relied on what Barbour terms the men 'of his own leding' (leading), which is to say the men who formed his own 'comitiva' of about 500 men. These would have been drawn chiefly from his tenants, but would also include men who had chosen to serve under his command over a period of years; they were his personal following who he could rely on to act together as a close-knit team of competent, confident and experienced soldiers.

Moray swiftly led his men down on to what Sir Thomas Grey (in *Scalacronica*) calls the 'good ground' – meaning firm land suitable for cavalry – and barred the way to the town. For Clifford and Beaumont, this was an unmissable opportunity and they actually drew their men back to allow the Scots to occupy a position on the flat plain before making an attempt to charge through them. As it turned out, this was not a wise move. The English cavalry failed repeatedly to break into the Scottish formation and, after a spell of hard fighting, found that they were actually being pushed backwards toward the River Forth. There had been examples in the past of determined and well-drilled infantry successfully repelling a cavalry attack, but this may have been the first medieval example of infantry successfully turning the attack against men-at-arms. After a prolonged fight, the English force eventually split into two parts, one heading for Stirling castle and the other retiring toward the main body of the army. Casualties had not been very high – according to Barbour the Scots did not lose a single man, which seems less than credible – but a number of prisoners were left behind, including Sir Thomas Grey.

Although the clashes of the first day had both been favourable to Robert, he was still not absolutely committed to giving battle. While he was deliberating his course of action, a third engagement took place at Cambuskenneth Abbey. Robert had selected the abbey as a repository for what Barbour describes as his own supplies. No doubt the abbey did house foodstuffs and the like, but it probably also housed Robert's records. The various lords and officers of the Crown who were obliged to furnish men and the different institutions charged with collecting and delivering the enormous quantities of food and other materials to keep the army in good shape would want to have receipts to show that they had fulfilled the demands made upon them. Because the troops were simply fulfilling the obligations required by national defence, Robert did not – so far as we can tell – have to pay them wages, but the costs would still have been considerable, and his officers,

39. *The sole remaining building of Cambuskenneth Abbey. During the night of 23/24 June, the Earl of Athol mounted an attack on King Robert's stores. Of the four actions of the battle, this is the only one of which the precise location can be identified without question.*

especially the chamberlain and the clerks of the Livery and the Spence (the financial departments of the Scottish Crown administrative structure), would have been busy men.

During the night of 23/24 June, the abbey was attacked by a party of troops under David Strathbogie, the Earl of Atholl. Atholl had been in King Robert's peace until very shortly before this, and had left Robert's side in anger because the king's brother, the Earl of Carrick, had jilted Atholl's sister. The attack was successful. A number of people were killed, including the elderly Sir William de Airth and various members of the royal household. The king's stores were destroyed and, in all probability, all the records of the army were lost along with them.

Barbour's account relates that on the night of 23 June, Robert had still not made a final decision about whether to offer battle the following day. So far the outcome had favoured his troops and there was something to be said for avoiding another engagement. The action at Cambuskenneth Abbey had been a blow, but a minor one, and an event that would not have any political, tactical or propaganda value. The other two actions had been definite successes. Neither had inflicted serious casualties on either side, but Robert could certainly claim to have had a good day. If he now chose to withdraw through the night it was unlikely that Edward would be able to make any effort to pursue the Scots until well into the next day, and it would be difficult, if not impossible, for the English army to close the distance that would separate them from the Scots. It would certainly be possible to detach a major portion of the cavalry, leaving the infantry behind, and catch up with the Scots within a day or perhaps two, but that would be risky policy: the event of 23 June had clearly demonstrated that the Scots were perfectly capable of dealing with unsupported cavalry attacks, and – assuming Robert withdrew into more challenging terrain – there would be some risk of suffering a major defeat.

On the other hand, if Robert did retreat, Edward would be able to relieve Stirling castle and would have an opportunity to install a new administration to take the place of the one that had been dislodged over the preceding years. These factors were not so significant as they might at first appear.

If Robert avoided battle, Edward would quickly run out of the money and supplies to keep his forces in the field and would inevitably have to disband at least a large proportion of the army. He might be able to keep Robert at bay with a smaller force, but again that would be a risky policy since Robert had demonstrated his tactical abilities in the past and might go on the offensive. The last thing Edward could afford was to be obliged to abandon his Scottish plans through force. Equally, although Stirling was a major prize, its value was limited unless Edward's administration could dominate the surrounding area to allow Stirling to be a centre of government. In the past, the occupation government had been able to maintain its authority through possession of an extensive chain of castles and peels throughout the country. This was no longer a viable option. Ever since his first successful campaigns, Robert had made a practice of slighting every stronghold he captured specifically to prevent them being used for this purpose. Most, if not all, of the castles and peels could be repaired, but only at considerable expense and Edward had neither the time nor the money for such an initiative.

The worst-case scenario for Robert – if he chose not to fight – was that Stirling would remain in English hands, but realistically, that would only be the case as long as Edward could keep a major army in Scotland. As soon as he withdrew his forces, the Scots could simply sweep back and Stirling would be in much the same position as it had been since spring 1314. Edward could certainly not afford to raise another army to return later in the year, and it was very doubtful that he would be able to do so the following year, plus he might well struggle to get the necessary political support. The greatest magnate in England had refused to give service in 1314 and was too powerful to be disciplined, and several others had had doubts about the 1314 campaign; indeed, there was some doubt about the wisdom of trying to conquer Scotland at all. As such, it might well have proven impossible to raise an army of any real stature for a campaign in 1315.

There was clearly a good case for Robert to avoid battle, but there were several factors that encouraged a more active stance. Although the two actions of 23 June had caused little material damage to Edward's army, the results inevitably had some deleterious effect on English morale and a very positive effect on the Scots. The effectiveness of the training of the last few weeks had been clearly demonstrated and the men were ready for a fight. Tactically, Robert's position was excellent. His forces were still out of sight of the enemy – his strength, organisation and dispositions were secure from view – whereas Edward's army was laid out on the plain below and could not make a move without being observed. Edward's army had not made a particularly rapid march from Northumberland, but were certainly not as fresh as they might be, while Robert's troops were well rested and had every confidence in their leaders. Only a fraction of the Scottish army had been engaged, and for many of the others this would be their first battle, but there would have been a high proportion of experienced men and they had become accustomed to winning. Robert was not in the way of offering battle and only did so when utterly confident of success. His men would have been aware of this and, therefore, Robert could be confident that they would trust him not to lead them into a fight if there was not an extremely high probability of victory. With a well-armed, well-trained, confident army, hungry for victory and in a highly advantageous tactical position, Robert had good reason to believe that this was an excellent opportunity to offer battle.

There were two other factors for Robert to bear in mind. During the late morning or early afternoon of 23 June, he had sent a party forward under Douglas to observe the English army; Douglas had reported back that the English army was enormous, but Robert now ensured that his own troops were told that the English were approaching in a state of disorder. Whether this was true was unimportant; what mattered was that his troops had been given another modest boost to their confidence and morale. The second factor was the appearance of a defector in the Scottish camp. Sir Alexander Seton had been an early supporter of the Bruce cause but the bulk of his property lay in Lothian and Robert's early failures meant that the occupation government there had been quite secure. Seton either had to accept the forfeiture of his family heritage or accept Plantagenet rule. Unsurprisingly, he had chosen the latter, but that does not mean that he had been happy to do so. Now he approached Robert, telling him of discontent and disorganisation in the English camp and that he was confident that if Robert mounted an attack he would win a great victory; he backed up his claim by offering to fight at Robert's side so that if there was any question of treachery Robert would be able to ensure that Seton would pay the traditional price.

Seton's defection was probably not a spur-of-the-moment decision. The Scots had taken the last major stronghold in Lothian a few months before, and although Robert had not yet been able to bring the area fully under his rule, clearly the writing was on the wall. Whether Seton really identified a lack of cohesion in the English army and whether it was the most significant factor in his change of heart is open to question, though presumably he would not have chosen to change sides in what was, essentially, a lull in the battle if he had been confident that Edward could lead his troops to a victory. All the same, his

Sir Alexander Seton

An early supporter of King Robert at the time of his attempt to take the throne, Seton soon entered the peace of Edward I and thereby retained his property and his local influence as a member of the Lothian political community. He re-joined the Bruce party on the night of 23/24 June, informing Robert that the English camp was in poor order and that there was an opportunity to strike a major blow in the morning.

defection was significant. Seton was not quite a member of the magnate class, but he was certainly a major figure in the local political community: a man whose name would be well known throughout the Scottish army, and doubtless Robert made sure that his transfer of allegiance was well advertised to the troops. For all these reasons – and doubtless others of which we are not aware – Robert decided to take the plunge and prepared his army for battle.

The Second Day

Traditionally, the action of 24 June has been described in terms of an English assault toward high ground which the Scots, arrayed in four great circles of spearmen, met with sturdy resolve until the English army was exhausted and broke into a headlong retreat. This is not in any degree borne out by the source material. Robert did not merely offer or accept battle, he actively forced it.

In the early dawn of 24 June – and dawn would have broken by 4 a.m. – Robert mustered his army for battle, probably in the area now covered by Stirling High School.

Far from waiting for the English to attack, he moved his columns quickly down to the flat ground and deployed them in three formations with a thin screen of archers to the front. Two of the major forces – under Carrick and Moray – formed up as broad formations some distance apart, with the third, under the king himself, between them and some distance to the rear. This did not pass unnoticed in the English camp. It seems likely that the English army was already preparing for the day, but that they were preparing for an advance toward the Scots, not to receive an attack. This is an issue of some significance. All in all, medieval armies moved in column and fought in line, and redeploying from one to the other was not something that could be easily or quickly achieved at the best of times, let alone in a relatively small area with the enemy in close proximity.

Once the Scots had made their way down on to the plain, they did a remarkable thing: they knelt down in prayer. Edward observed this and asked – perhaps in jest – if the Scots were kneeling to beg for mercy, only to be told that if they were, it was for mercy from God, not him. This is an incident that has generally been seen as a demonstration of medieval piety, and doubtless that had significance to the men on the battlefield, but there may have been a tactical value. The broad and relatively shallow spear formations would only be effective if the 'dressing' (the regularity of the ranks and files) of the troops was kept in good order. If the majority of the troops were kneeling down, it would be a great help to what we would now call the 'junior leaders' of the units to move up and down the ranks quickly, ensuring that every man was firmly in line with his neighbours, and that the unit as a whole was in the best possible order.

The Scottish army was now deployed on a front of a thousand yards or more between the courses of the Pelstream and the Bannock burns and, at most, a mile from the main body of the English. As they marched eastward toward the enemy, the screen of archers to their front soon came into action against a similar screen of English archers, who had presumably been positioned to obstruct the sort of night attack that Edward and his subordinates had anticipated. The Scots archers seem to have made little impression on their opponents and were either quickly driven off or had instructions to make a demonstration rather than to press the fight. Either way, they had fulfilled their purpose by preventing the English archers from disrupting the advancing spearmen, because by the time the Scottish archers made their exit, the schiltroms were too close for comfort, as far as the English archers were concerned, and they made a quick exit to avoid being overwhelmed.

While this opening phase of the engagement was taking place, at least one senior English commander was taking action. The Earl of Gloucester managed to organise a body of cavalry and mount a charge against the nearest Scottish schiltrom under the Earl of Carrick. Gloucester may have hoped that the Scots would crumble at the first blow or that his attack would at least cause the Scots to pause and perhaps give the rest of the English army an opportunity to complete redeployment for battle, but this was not to be the case. His attack ground to a halt against Carrick's spearmen and his men were driven back toward the main body of the army. As the distance between the two forces shrank in the face of the Scottish advance, it proved impossible for Gloucester's men to retire and regroup for a second charge, but Gloucester himself was unable to influence the situation since he had been killed at the outset.

The repulse of this first attempt to stop the Scots in their tracks doubtless put something of a dent in the morale of the rest of the English army, and the scattered and disorganised remnant of Gloucester's command probably made it more difficult for other English commanders to get their troops into good order to receive the Scottish attack.

40. A well-intentioned re-enactor in the tradition of Brigadoon *meets* Braveheart; *however, neither kilts nor two-handed swords have any relevance to the fourteenth century.*

On the other side of the battlefield, Moray pressed forward to contact and some hard fighting ensued, but again it proved impossible to stop the Scottish advance. Clearly things were not going well for Edward's army, since they were now being forced backwards in increasingly poor order toward their campsite, with an inevitable effect on morale and cohesion. This was compounded by the advance of the third Scottish formation, which the king led forward between the commands of Carrick and Moray so that a complete front was formed, stretching from the Pelstream to the Bannock burns. As the army advanced, effectively as a single body, there was less and less room to organise a counterstroke and, even if an adequate force could be gathered, the opportunity to deliver a blow to the inner flanks of Moray or Carrick's divisions had been lost.

Nevertheless, the battle was, as yet, far from lost. The Scots were having a hard fight of it and were still heavily outnumbered. There is some doubt about the next development in the battle since it is recorded in only one account. According to Barbour, Edward – or one of his subordinates – was able to get a grip on the situation and bring a large body of archers into action on one flank. However effective it might be against cavalry or close-combat infantry, a schiltrom was a very easy target for archery, and casualties started to mount quickly. Robert had foreseen the possibility that he might need a force to intervene at a critical juncture and had organised a reserve of cavalry under Sir Robert Keith, who now charged into the flank of the archers and scattered them. This force is generally described as being 'light' cavalry, but that assumption rests on one word in one line from Barbour's poem, in which he tells his audience that the horses were 'lecht'. Whether this means that they were not the strong and fast destriers and chargers generally favoured by men-at-arms is open to question. Barbour may simply have meant that the horses were fresh and mettlesome, or he may only have included the term to complete the metre (rhythm) of the line. In practice, it would make very little difference to the men of the receiving end of the charge. Any body of armoured cavalry that broke into a formation or archers was almost certain to rout their opponents with ease.

The case against this part of the action happening at all, let alone as Barbour describes it, is worth examining. English chroniclers state that the entire Scottish army – including the king, who carried his spear among the rank and file – served on foot. On the other hand, it is most unlikely that Robert did not arrange for horses to be readily available so that any opportunity to pursue the enemy could be exploited or so that he and others might have a chance of making their escape if the battle went badly. One English writer, Geoffrey Baker, writing about thirty years after the battle, informs us that the English archers were unable to make an effective contribution to the fighting as they were in the rearmost divisions of the army and could not shoot for fear of hitting their own comrades.

PALFREY

A 'riding' horse, as opposed to a charger for battle. A palfrey was not a breed but a type, and might be little more than a nag or, on the other hand, a very expensive, cherished piece of horseflesh. King Robert was riding his palfrey when he killed Sir Henry de Bohun in single combat. It has been suggested – even stated – that the animal was named 'Ferrand'; however, the term crops up frequently in horse valuations and simply means 'grey'.

DESTRIERS

A type rather than a specific breed of animal, destriers were not terribly common and most men-at-arms were content to have a courser, which was cheaper and easier to replace. Contrary to common belief, they were not particularly large animals, generally between 14 and 15 hands tall and very powerfully built.

This does make some tactical sense. If, as the Lanercost chronicle states, both armies were 'arrayed' at dawn on 24 June, it would be perfectly viable for the close-combat troops to be at the front of the army, given that Edward and his commander expected to have to locate and then advance on the Scots. Had that been the case, the logical approach to deployment would have been to ensure that the archers were not vulnerable to an advance by the Scots, but would be available for deployment once the Scots had been pinned in a particular position, as had been the case at Falkirk.

For Barbour, the rout of the English archers was a crucial event in the battle, since they now fled toward the main body of the army and caused even greater disorganisation, which, as the Scottish schiltroms pushed on, induced a degree of panic. All of this was compounded by a lack of room to manoeuvre. The two streams that had given Edward's army the vital supply of fresh water for both men and beasts, and had afforded his campsite and initial deployment area some security from night attacks, now proved to be a liability rather than an asset. Neither stream was necessarily an insuperable barrier to an individual who could carefully pick his way across the least challenging parts of the burns, but both were rather more significant streams than they are today and undoubtedly presented a major obstacle to a body of troops. It is important to bear in mind that there was only a very short period of time from the arrival of the Scots on the plain to the point when both armies were heavily engaged right across their respective fronts. Although the great majority of the Scottish army was now in action, a large portion of the English troops were not yet in the fight. However, extricating a worthwhile force from the main body of the army and then getting them across the Bannock or the Pelstream, with a view to delivering an attack on the flanks or rear of the enemy, would have taken some time and was not, in any case, a very practical proposition. It is not clear that any of Edward's officers tried to effect such a manoeuvre, but even if they had, there was every likelihood that Robert would have been afforded ample time to take action against any threat to his flanks, or that by the time such a force had been gathered and deployed, the battle would already have been lost.

There is no way of knowing whether leaders in Edward's army tried to effect a flanking move against the Scots, but if they did, it certainly did not lead to anything. As the Scots pressed forward greater numbers of English troops lost heart and started to make to the rear passing through the camp area, only to find their way blocked by the Bannock burn. Thomas Grey (*Scalacronica*) informs us that many tried to escape by the route that had brought them to the battlefield, only to fall foul of what he calls the 'stinking ditch' and to drown, get crushed underfoot or be picked off by the Scots as they floundered in the muddy stream bed. Others retreated directly away from the Scottish advance and soon found themselves on the western bank of the River Forth. The Forth is still subject to the tide as far Stirling; at low tide the expanse of water is not great, but the exposed banks are deep, sticky mud and would be a challenge to anyone, let alone a man encumbered by even the lightest armour.

At a late point in the battle, another incident may have occurred to undermine the English army. According to Barbour, the grooms, servants and various camp followers of the Scottish army had been stationed well way from the battlefield with instructions to remain there until the fighting was finished. Seeing that the English were defeated, these men – and doubtless women too – gathered behind a leader of their own number and rushed down to the plain to make a contribution to the fighting. There is some doubt about their involvement, but the 'small folk', as Barbour calls them, would certainly have existed – medieval armies required a considerable number of skilled and semi-skilled ancillary workers – and it is hard to imagine that they would not have seized an opportunity to take part in the plundering of the English camp and baggage trains. What is less likely is that their participation had any effect on the outcome of the battle. Even if they were only a mile or two from the action – and it is unlikely to have been less – if they started out toward the fight at the point when the English army started to disintegrate, they can hardly have arrived before the final outcome had been decided.

As it became all too apparent that the Scots had won the day, Edward threw himself into the fight but was dragged away from combat by the men who were responsible for the safety of his person, including Sir Giles d'Argentan. The problem now was where to take him. As Edward's standard was seen leaving the field, those English troops who were still in action finally gave up the struggle and either attempted to surrender or to follow after those who were already attempting to escape. Getting away from the battlefield was, however, easier said than done. To the north there was the Pelstream burn, but there was also, assuming that Barbour's account is valid, the force of Scottish men-at-arms who had scattered the English archers.

A strong body of men might make a safe passage there if they could retain enough cohesion to deter the Scottish horse, but it would be a risky option for a small group or an individual, and any move northward would lead away from the English border and security. To the east there was the River Forth – not a huge river, but any kind of water course is a major obstacle to a man in armour. Furthermore, the banks of the Forth at that point are very broad and soft, so crossing the river is actually much more difficult than it might seem. To the south there was the Bannock burn. Like the Pelstream, it is not a large river, but like the Forth the banks are soft and muddy. According to Thomas Grey's *Scalacronica*, this was the main line of retreat and large numbers of English troops 'fell back on the ditch of Bannock burn tumbling one over the other'.

King Edward's party forced their way across the Pelstream burn and headed for Stirling castle as the nearest place of safety. Any hope that this might prove an adequate sanctuary was short-lived. The garrison commander, Sir Philip Moubray (the man who had made the surrender pact with the Earl of Carrick three months earlier), informed Edward that although he was prepared to take Edward into the castle and offer him what protection he could, the plain fact was that he was obliged to surrender the castle to the Scots at the earliest opportunity. Even if he refused to honour the agreement, for all practical purposes defending the castle was a lost cause. The Scots would simply restore the siege that they had lifted back in April and the garrison would be starved out or stormed long before there was any prospect of a new army being raised in England to rescue the king; in fact, with Edward holed up in Stirling, there was little prospect of a relief force being raised at all.

Clearly Edward either had to attempt to make his way home to England or face surrendering to King Robert, which would be an unmitigated disaster. The prestige of Edward – and of English kingship in general – would be very badly damaged, which would likely have consequences for his credibility among his subjects in France, as well as finally destroying any standing he might retain among Scots who had accepted Plantagenet rule. Additionally, there would be the political and financial cost of obtaining his liberty. Undoubtedly, any terms would have to include a complete and unreserved acceptance of Robert's kingship and solemn oaths never to attack Scotland again, but there would also be the matter of a ransom, which might well run into hundreds of thousands of pounds. Edward could be sure of his personal safety – Robert was hardly going to execute him – but equally he could hardly expect to be set free before a ransom had been agreed and at least a substantial proportion delivered.

The chances of making a successful escape were actually quite good. Edward was not alone, but was surrounded by a large party – probably some hundreds – of men-at-arms. Many of these would have been the men of personal retinue, joined by those who had followed the royal banner on their own initiative when Edward left the battlefield. Between them they formed a fairly formidable force. The decision was made to pass round the western side of the New Park and King's Park and then to proceed to nearest point of safety.

Down on the plain, where the battle was finally coming to a close, Edward's party was observed leaving Stirling and King Robert dispatched a force of men-at-arms under Douglas in the hope of capturing Edward. Douglas took to the pursuit with his usual determination, but his party was too small to force an action against Edward's following. During the pursuit Douglas encountered Sir Laurence Abernethy, who had brought a party of men-at-arms – eighty strong, according to Barbour – to join the English army.

Ever the realist, Abernethy quickly decided that the Plantagenet cause was lost and joined Douglas in the chase. However, even with these unexpected reinforcements, Douglas could not risk an engagement and settled for picking up those English stragglers who fell behind the rest of the party. Barbour describes a hell-for-leather ride through the counties of the south-east as far as Dunbar, where the earl, still firmly opposed to the Bruce party, admitted Edward and provided him with a boat to take him to Berwick, where he would be in no immediate danger. In fact, the pursuit was probably a more leisurely business than Barbour describes, since the horses of both sides would soon have collapsed with exhaustion if they had been driven to trot, let alone gallop over such a long distance.

While Edward made his way to Dunbar, at least one of his commanders was trying to rescue what he could from the fight. Aymer de Valence, Earl of Pembroke, gathered a force of infantry and men-at-arms that was strong enough to discourage any serious interference and marched south. Others were less fortunate. A party escaped as far as Bothwell, where the commander of the garrison claimed that he could only accommodate the leaders of the group, who

RANSOMS

Throughout most of the war, a man who was captured could secure his release by payment of a ransom. Ransoms were normally set at a level that the prisoner could reasonably be expected to raise and payment terms might be spread over some years. Ransoms were usually a matter between the captor and his captive, though it was not unusual for the Crown to receive a portion of the money since the captor would – as a general rule – be serving in the king's army.

then entered the castle only to be taken prisoner. For the rest of the army, the situation was more than bleak: it was desperate. No doubt many managed to escape the battlefield only to be killed or captured as they fled south. Of those who did not die on the field, many were drowned or crushed trying to escape across the Bannock or the Forth; many more surrendered – some apparently even to peasant women – in the hope that their value as prisoners for ransom would help to keep them alive.

Robert certainly took a major gamble at Bannockburn, and two of the greatest Scottish medieval historians, Professors Ranald Nicholson and Geoffrey Barrow (and others in his wake), have concluded that it was a gamble he should not have taken. His authority as king largely depended on his military success. Some men had joined his cause through family traditions, patriotic convictions or coercion, but for many Robert seemed to offer the best prospect for delivering what medieval writers called 'good lordship': secure and steady government that could be relied upon to provide stability and prosperity. A single defeat on the battlefield would utterly compromise his credibility even if he escaped, and if he was captured he would certainly face execution.

All battles involve risk, but Robert had taken pains to load the dice very firmly in his own favour. Edward II had made reference to taking an army to 'our castle of Stirling' as early as October 1313, but that was not the sole target and he might easily have chosen a different course for his expedition, or at least one that encompassed other objectives. The clear challenge to Stirling that was created by the pact between the Earl of Carrick and Sir Philip Moubray did not completely force Edward's hand, but it would have been a sign of weakness had he not made a serious effort to relieve the garrison before midsummer. If anything, the pact gave Edward a clear target,

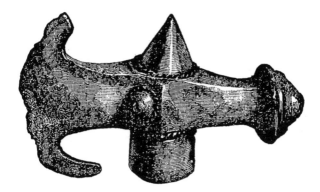

41. The head of a battle-hammer allegedly recovered from Bannockburn battlefield.

since Robert would have to make some sort of demonstration of opposition. With any luck, Robert would muster a significant force and be brought to battle.

For Robert, the Stirling area had very real advantages as a place to obstruct, if not engage, an English invasion. The strategic value lay in the fact that Stirling is right in the centre of the country and had, by medieval standards, excellent communications in all directions. Since the castle garrison was completely contained, supplies could be brought up the Forth in barges to within a couple of miles of the army's training and concentration area without fear of interruption. Additionally, the first bridge over the Forth was at Stirling. In a previous expedition, Edward I had built a pontoon bridge over the Forth and it was not impossible that Edward II might do the same. If so, news of it would come to Robert long before it was completed; this would allow him to march his army to block Edward's crossing on the north bank. There were also tactical attractions: the terrain had good potential for a defensive action on the wooded high ground of the New Park, where Edward's superiority in cavalry and archers would be less significant, and there was also ample dry, open terrain where Robert could drill large bodies of spearmen.

Robert's troops were well motivated, confident, well armed and well trained. He and his commanders were totally familiar with the terrain. They had developed a series of combat manoeuvres and had instilled them into the troops, but above all, Robert had planned thoroughly. His army was positioned so that if the English gained the upper hand in the pre-battle manoeuvres, he would be able to withdraw into territory that favoured his own forces over those of his enemy, but he was also ready to seize an opportunity to accept, offer or, as it turned out, force battle on his enemy if the circumstances were favourable.

If the risks of defeat were enormous, the advantages to be gained from victory were even greater. If Edward could be decisively beaten on the battlefield, Robert's own prestige would be secured and the final significant English-held stronghold in central Scotland would be taken without a blow being struck. Additionally, there was the prospect of taking some prominent prisoners who could then be exchanged for the various Scots in English captivity. However, there was also the question of the risks of not giving battle. Robert had been assiduous in regularly demanding military service from his subjects even though the great majority of his troops never saw action. If he continually called out men but never took them to battle the exercise would come to be seen as a waste of time and effort. In the summer of 1314, he raised the biggest force of his reign to date and avoiding battle might well have had a detrimental effect on the morale of his troops: what was the point of all that training if the king was afraid to commit himself to the sort of battle that could decide his own future and that of his kingdom? However hazardous the decision to force a battle might have been, the decision paid off handsomely and Robert's status, both at home and abroad, was hugely enhanced by his victory.

AFTER THE BATTLE

Edward's flight to Stirling castle and then to Dunbar and on to Berwick ended the campaign of 1314. The financial cost had been enormous and there was nothing to show for it. Raising another army immediately would have been an impossible strain on the economy and the loss of so many members of the English political community was a further barrier. The lords and gentry who were now dead on the battlefield or prisoners in Scotland would not be available to raise troops, fulfil command and administration roles or serve as men-at-arms. The communities of northern England had provided the bulk of the infantry and could not be expected to fill the ranks of a new army, so men would have had to be recruited from the southern counties, which would weaken defences against raids or even invasion from France.

A number of major lords had refused to serve in 1314 and several of those who had were now prisoners. Many had been killed and even if their heirs were of military age, many of them would have had their hands filled with the business of establishing their leadership within their communities, and very few of them would have had any significant command experience. Additionally, the mere fact of the defeat – and its scale – was hardly an encouraging factor. Few men would have retained any confidence in Edward as a commander, and the situation did not reflect well on those of his senior subordinates who had escaped death or capture. For some, there would have been a big question mark over the value of pursuing the war at all, given the costs, the risks and the potential benefits of victory. There were probably some men of a more pious nature who saw the hand of God at work and concluded that the war was not justified. Beyond that, there was the question of whether the war could be won. Robert had managed to survive every initiative taken against him, but even if he could be killed and the Scots defeated in battle, was it not likely that the Scots would find another captain to champion their cause? Edward Bruce would almost certainly take on the challenge and, whether he did or not, Edward Balliol might well do the same.

None of these factors would be enough necessarily to dissuade Edward II from raising another army, but there was the very real possibility that it, too, might be defeated. Additionally, even if a victory could be achieved, what was the benefit? A relatively modest number of men might make good the grants of lands, offices and titles bestowed on them by Edward I, but it was abundantly clear that Scotland could not be garrisoned by a few handfuls of men in scattered castles and peels. If an occupation government was to be successful, it would have to be secured by very large forces and at enormous costs. Most, if not all, of the castles that had been slighted by Robert and his lieutenants would have to be repaired and the garrisons would have to be paid and supplied from English resources. It was not even clear that the manpower to provide the garrisons could be recruited. From 1297 to 1314, it had been possible to enlist men-at-arms and archers from Scottish communities and to extract the knight service of several counties to provide soldiers to man the castles and peels. This was likely to be much harder to achieve in the wake of such a major defeat. There were certainly some men available: Scottish men who had not entered the peace of King Robert and had become exiles, but there were not enough of them to provide the sort of active garrisons that would be needed to impose Edward's rule. Furthermore, Robert had established a general practice of accepting such men into his peace on reasonably attractive terms, but also made it clear that there was a limited window of opportunity and that men who did not enter his peace – at the price of abandoning any landholding from or allegiance to the kings of England – would be forfeited forever. Given the choice of submitting to Robert, accepting his kingship and being reinstated to some or even all of one's heritage, or spending who knew how long as a pensioner of the English Crown in the hopes that one day Plantagenet or even Balliol kingship would be restored, it would hardly be surprising if a high proportion of these 'disinherited' lords sought to make their peace with the Bruce party.

All in all, the events of 1314 left English military prestige and confidence severely shaken. This was a major issue given Edward's relationship with France and the challenges to English authority in Ireland and Wales. The failure of the campaign also generated profound dismay in the communities of northern England. If Edward could not protect his subjects in Northumberland, Cumberland and Westmorland, there was always the risk that the political communities in those areas would look to someone who could provide them with better lordship: King Robert. Although Robert always maintained that he had no ambitions to conquer English territory, there were clear symptoms of a collapse in northern confidence in Edward's kingship. In the years after

Bannockburn several landholders in northern English counties, having paid the ransoms that Robert demanded for refraining from destruction, approached Robert for legal decisions or to have their charters confirmed.

There was also increasing cause for concern to other communities further south. Part of the price for peace in the northern English counties was Robert's insistence on free passage for his troops from ransomed communities, which potentially gave his raids much greater range. From Robert's point of view, the repeated incursions into England were not simply a matter of keeping his army in good condition – though clearly that was a significant factor – or even with easing his own financial problems. He entertained hopes that such activity would eventually force Edward to open negotiations for a proper peace agreement, but he misread the situation. Quite simply, Edward was just not that concerned about the communities of northern England.

Edward was neither willing nor able to abandon Scottish ambitions; to do so would be an admission of defeat and would be seen as throwing away the accomplishments of his father. This was hardly realistic as his father had, in fact, failed to defeat the Scots, but he had achieved at least an appearance of nearing his objective in 1304–05. At the time of Edward's death in 1307, Robert Bruce was an insignificant threat and, superficially at least, Scottish independence as a political concept was very close to being extinguished – at least in English public perception.

Edward II inherited the Scottish war from his father; the war was Edward I's project and over the years it became something of a fixation, and – for Edward II – to some extent it became a means of deflecting attention from internal problems. To a degree, it had served a similar function for Edward I. In the late 1290s, England was sometimes on the brink of civil war and focusing attention on the Scottish situation helped to give a common purpose to the differing factions in domestic politics.

By 1314, the desire to conquer Scotland had become so thoroughly entrenched that it was virtually impossible to abandon it. Massive sums of money had been committed and there would be nothing to show for so much effort if Edward simply accepted Robert's kingship. Bannockburn did not bring the war to an end: Edward would mount further expeditions into Scotland, but he was never able to bring the Scots to battle on their own soil. However, his forces suffered defeats on English soil and this did nothing to improve Edward's standing among his nobles or the wider community.

The economic damage incurred from Robert's operations in northern England did not have a major direct effect on Edward's personal income, but the raids did lead to depopulation as

42. Letter patent of John Balliol, acknowledging the feudal superiority of Edward I.

people moved south to avoid the conflict; this, in turn, made it more difficult to recruit adequate numbers for English operations in Scotland, so the cost in manpower and money had to be found from counties in the south, and that did not help to make Edward popular with his subjects. Additionally, the prospects for his Scottish pensioners became increasingly bleak. Their number was not great, but it was not trivial either, and they became a steady drain on Edward's treasury. The same applied to men who had been granted Scottish estates and offices. Clearly, they now had no realistic chance of gaining their lands or salaries any time soon, but many of them had to be compensated for their losses with grants of land in England or money from Edward's treasury.

In addition to the internal dissent that was encouraged by Bannockburn, Edward's prestige abroad – which was never very strong in the first place – was seriously undermined. Bannockburn gave Robert political and military credibility, particularly in France and the Low Countries, who could now more safely resume trade on the sort of level that had pertained in the years before the war.

Nevertheless, one area of success was in the diplomatic struggle. Edward was able to dissuade the pope from lifting the sentence of excommunication from Robert, which had been decreed for his murder of Sir John Comyn of Badenoch in 1306. However, it is questionable whether any of Edward's subjects really saw that as a victory of any consequence.

For Robert, the victory brought any number of rewards. His control of Scotland was complete and effectively unquestioned; the men who might have opposed him were either dead or exiles in England. However, strictly speaking, he was still not universally regarded as the legitimate king. Although John Balliol had abdicated in 1296 and then some years later had forsworn any and all rights in Scotland, he had done so under

43. The seal of John Balliol.

duress and therefore there was some doubt about the validity
of his actions, and even more doubt about whether he could
legitimately give away the rights of his heir, Edward Balliol. As
long as Balliol *fils* lived, there would always be a risk that a
pro-Balliol movement might arise and attempt to topple Robert
in order to put the legitimate heir on the throne. This might
have seemed a little far-fetched in the immediate afterglow of
such a stunning victory or in the wake of Robert's successful
campaigns in England, but the principle of legitimacy in
inheritance was of enormous importance in medieval societies.
A mere six years after Bannockburn there was a plot to murder
King Robert. Barbour points to Sir John de Soulis as the man
that the conspirators were seeking to put on the throne, but he
also reports that a band of 360 men-at-arms had gathered at

Berwick to carry out a coup once Robert had been dispatched. These men were undoubtedly drawn from the ranks of those who had lost their lands through their opposition to the Bruce party, and their intention was to make Edward Balliol king in Robert's place. The plot was a complete failure and many of the conspirators were tried and executed, the remainder fleeing to England or France, but clearly there was still life in the Balliol cause.

Robert faced other problems. An attempt to take the war to Ireland initially looked like it might bear fruit and even result in Edward Bruce becoming king of an independent Ireland, but in due course the attempt fizzled out and Edward Bruce himself was killed in action at Faughart on 4 October 1318.

Despite these setbacks, Robert was able to conduct the affairs of the kingdom with considerable success and there was a general economic recovery despite some very poor years for agriculture. In one sense, the military picture was relatively bright. Control over the more pastoral areas of Scotland allowed Robert to recruit larger numbers of men-at-arms, which helped to make his raids into England more effective. Douglas and Moray were able to gain victories against the forces of Edward II, but the range of their operations was limited. They could make forays as far south as Huntingdonshire, but could not really threaten Edward's political power base in the south of England. Robert's armies could win the battles, but securing a permanent peace continued to elude him.

In the meantime, as he pursued his military and diplomatic campaigns, Robert was able to devote himself to the business of running the country. Like any medieval king, his domestic priorities revolved around ensuring that his rule was firmly established throughout the realm and encouraging economic development. Possession of all of Scotland's ports allowed a resumption of the wool trade. Wool was the most significant export of both England and Scotland. Of all the tradeable wool sold in late medieval Western Europe, something approaching 80 per cent of it was produced in England and virtually all of the rest came from Scotland. Wool was not the only export, but it was the only one subject to export taxes, and, as such, there is more evidence about the wool trade than any other commodity; however, that does not mean that other trade goods were insignificant. Furs, hides, timber, salt, honey and grain were all of some consequence, but none came remotely close to wool in terms of generating income either for merchants of for the Crown. Export is generally accompanied by import, and medieval Scotland was no exception. Iron was in short supply locally and a great deal had to be brought in from abroad, but a large proportion of the imported material consisted of luxury goods. Of these, wine was probably the most significant as there was no domestic production whatsoever. The same applied to spices, which appear frequently – and in remarkably large quantities – in medieval records. The most popular spices seem to have been cumin, pepper and galingale (a form of ginger), which rather suggests that the Scottish devotion to curry (chicken tikka masala was possibly invented to appeal to Scottish tastes) is not a modern phenomenon.

In the immediate aftermath of Bannockburn, and intermittently for some years thereafter, war itself was a major source of economic activity. The ransoms that Robert demanded from English towns and counties helped to ease his financial difficulties, though it would seem probable that a great deal of that income was spent on wages for his soldiers. The forces that Moray, Douglas and Robert himself led into England maintained very high standards of discipline and that could only have been maintained if the troops were rewarded with cash rather than by being allowed to take plunder. Even so, there were opportunities. The men captured at Bannockburn, at Myton and Byland, and at scores of other actions could only obtain their liberty by paying ransoms to their captors, so a good many Scottish soldiers became personally wealthy through their service in the field.

Imposing law and order was a major task for Robert and his lieutenants. The war had produced extensive social dislocation. There were a good many landless men who had turned to robbery and extortion to make a living. This was not a uniquely Scottish problem. Even in peacetime, the business of hunting down bandits was part of the fabric of life in every country in Europe, but it was something that flourished in periods of conflict due to the fact that the class of men who would normally have responsibility for ensuring peace and good order were generally more focused on the business of conducting a war. In peacetime, the knight service owed to the Crown and to figures of local authority could be committed to the task of suppressing bands of criminals, but in war the service was needed elsewhere.

Eventually it would be a series of internal political crises in England that would give Robert the treaty of 'final peace' that he desired. Edward was never able to exert the level of control over his nobility that his father had mostly been able to achieve, but a mixture of social conservatism and divisions in his opposition kept him on the throne long after he had demonstrated that the task of being a competent king was beyond his abilities. A chain of revolts and refusals to give service undermined his authority and in May 1325 he made a huge tactical error in sending his eldest son, the future Edward III, to act as his proxy in giving homage to the King of France for the Duchy of Gascony. Edward's French queen, Isabella, had already travelled to France to negotiate a peace treaty, but now, with custody of her son, she refused to return at Edward's request. In September the following year she

PEACE (OF KING EDWARD OR KING ROBERT)

An individual changing sides from one party to the other was considered to have 'entered the peace' of the king and was thereby pardoned his previous resistance – though normally for a price.

mounted an invasion and within a short time Edward was not only defeated, but imprisoned.

In January 1327, Edward was formally charged with an enormous range of failures, including the 'loss' of Scotland, though in fact neither he nor his father had ever really secured their rule there in the first place. He agreed to abdicate in favour of his son and was placed in prison for life, but as long as he lived there was always the chance that his supporters might set him free and restore his kingship. Edward may not have been a very successful king, but the principle of legitimacy that constituted such a threat to Robert Bruce from the Balliol family was just as strong in medieval England as it was in Scotland. Additionally, although Edward III was now king in theory, he was still too young to rule in person and the government of the land lay with Isabella and her lover, Roger Mortimer.

The crisis in England had a bearing on the situation vis-à-vis Scotland. After years of demanding ransoms from communities in the north of England, the nearest thing to peace that Robert had been able to force from Edward II had been a truce to last for thirteen years – the medieval equivalent of a political problem being 'kicked into the long grass'. King Robert now took the view that the truce had been a personal arrangement between himself and Edward, and that his death rendered that arrangement null and void. Accordingly, Moray and Douglas renewed their operations. Robert may have hoped that Isabella and Mortimer, preoccupied with their own difficulties, might be brought to the peace table. Arguable, but they simply proved to have the same attitude to Scotland as Edward and were prepared to ignore the plight of the northern counties. However, since part of the rationale offered for forcing Edward II to abdicate had been the fact that he had failed to conquer Scotland, they could hardly afford simply to surrender to Robert's demands for recognition of his kingship and a full and lasting peace. Additionally, abandoning the conquest of Scotland might further alienate the young Edward III, since he – and, by this time, quite a sizeable proportion of the political community and the people as a whole – had come to see Scotland as part of the birthright of English kings. Accordingly, they raised an army and sent it north with the young Edward at its head.

The campaign was a disaster. The Scottish and English armies traipse up and down Weardale in the rain. There was very little actual fighting and the Scots had the better of what there was. At one particularly dispiriting juncture, Edward III was very fortunate to avoid capture. The Weardale campaign was a humiliation for Edward and for the English army in general; it also emptied the treasury and dissipated what little political capital Isabella and Mortimer still had.

The moment had come to make peace. King Robert's health was failing and he was anxious to reach agreement; his terms were generous, including a payment of £30,000 – an absolutely gigantic sum for those days – for the construction of an abbey dedicated to praying for the souls of those who had died on both sides. He may or may not have been aware that the money would go straight into Isabella and Mortimer's pockets, but he had made the right sort of gesture by providing the money for the stated purpose.

THE LEGACY

Victory in battle – and on such a dramatic scale – enhanced Robert's prestige and credibility to an enormous degree, though strictly speaking he was still a usurper. There remained a considerable sympathy throughout Scotland for the Balliol party, but Robert was now clearly seen as being the best bet for defending Scottish interests against English occupation. Whether any real sympathy had ever truly existed for the Plantagenets as rulers of Scotland in the years after 1296 is highly questionable, but by the end of June 1314 it had utterly evaporated and would never be a serious factor in Scottish political life again, though it would enjoy a brief, superficial and highly localised resurgence in 1333–35.

Robert had hoped that the peace of 1328 would be secured through the marriage of his son to Edward II's daughter, but Edward III was quite willing to put aside the interests of his sister if it meant the conquest of even part of Scotland, and gave support, initially covertly, to Edward Balliol, who, not unreasonably, was prepared to give homage to Edward III in exchange for being put on the Scottish throne.

The treaty of 1328 utterly forbade Edward II from giving support to anyone who might contest the kingship of Robert I;

Angus Og MacDonald

One of King Robert's most important followers, his support was especially significant in the early stages of Robert's campaigns to make himself king. It is not clear that he was present at Bannockburn; only Barbour suggests that he was. He may instead have been deployed to the west coast to prevent Irish troops from joining the English army.

44. The Pilkington Jackson statue of Robert I at the National Trust for Scotland's Bannockburn Visitor Centre.

45. *The nineteenth-century brass effigy of King Robert from his burial place at Dunfermline Abbey; in the 1330s the tombs of both King Robert and his queen – Elizabeth de Burgh – were destroyed by English troops.*

nevertheless, the only possible candidate, Edward Balliol, was not mentioned by name. By July 1332, Balliol had raised a small army consisting of English mercenaries and those men (collectively known as the Disinherited) who had lost lands and titles by opposing King Robert. The army seems to have numbered less than 2,000 men and it took more than eighty ships to carry them to Scotland, but the real leader of the expedition was not Edward, but Henry de Beaumont. The expedition initially enjoyed great success. The Scots had lost their most experienced leaders: Moray had died, possibly poisoned by an English spy, and Douglas had been killed in battle on crusade in Spain. The new leaders failed to co-ordinate their efforts and for a few months Balliol faced limited opposition; however, at Christmas he was driven out of Scotland and was lucky to escape with his life.

Edward III now took a hand in the business and endeavoured to put Edward Balliol on the Scottish throne as a client king in exchange for most of the southern counties of Scotland, which were to be ceded permanently to the English Crown. Despite initial success and a massive military effort, which would be a drain on English resources for decades, the two Edwards failed to make much headway. On 30 November 1335, the Scots scored a major victory at Culblean and, although they suffered numerous setbacks, the war continued to run their way. By 1340, if not before, Edward III had effectively abandoned any hope of achieving the conquest that had eluded his father and his grandfather, and had resorted to an outpost policy of maintaining a modest number of garrisons in Scottish castles as a means of keeping the Scots occupied and preventing them from making a more substantial contribution to the French side of what we now call the Hundred Years War.

This, then, was the sour fruit of Edward I's ambition. Only a few decades previously the plan to marry Edward I's son to

Alexander III's granddaughter and bring about a dynastic union had not been met with disapproval among the Scottish political community, though inevitably it would have led to a diminution of the Scottish state. By choosing a policy of armed occupation, Edward had destroyed the healthy relationship between the two countries that had existed before the Great Cause or Competition of 1291–92 and had laid the foundations for a bitter enmity on both sides built on an unbounded suspicion of all things English among the Scots and a condescending resentment of all things Scottish among the English.

ORDERS OF BATTLE

The Scots

Commander: Robert I

King Robert

First spear formation: possibly in excess of 2,000 spearmen

Edward Bruce, Earl of Carrick

Second spear formation: at least 1,500–2,000 spearmen

Thomas Randolph, Earl of Moray

Third spear formation: c. 1,500–2,000 men

Robert Keith Earl Marischal

500 men-at-arms (Barbour)

Sir James Douglas

Commanded the pursuit of Edward II to Dunbar

Archers

No information about their commander
500–1,000 men

The English

Commander: Edward II

Cavalry

2,500 men-at-arms divided into four separate commands, one
– rather larger than the others – nominally led by the king, and
three under senior nobles

Infantry

Writs for conscription requested: 21,000 infantry; it is
reasonable to conclude 12,000–17,000 men in total

FURTHER READING

Ayton, A., *Knights and their Warhorses*.

Barrell, A.D.M., *Medieval Scotland*.

Barrow, G.W.S., *Robert the Bruce*.

Brown, C., *Bannockburn 1314*.

Coss, P., *The Knight in Medieval England*.

Gardiner, S.R., *Atlas of English History*.

Keene, M., *Chivalry*.

MacNamee, C., *Robert Bruce*.

Oman, C.W.C., *A History of the Art of War in the Middle Ages*.

Prestwich, M., *Armies and Warfare in the Middle Ages: The English Experience*.

———, *The Three Edwards*.

INDEX

Abernethy, Sir Laurence, 126–7

Airth, Sir William, 112

Alexander III, King of Scotland, 8, 19, 21, 23–6, 29, 115, 148

Baker, Geoffrey, 121

Balliol, Edward, 34–5, 38, 48, 133

Balliol, John, King of Scotland, 8, 19, 25–7, 33, 42, 136–7

Barbour, John, 36, 44, 48, 53, 57–9, 84–8, 90–1, 107, 109–10, 112, 120–2, 124–7, 138

Beaumont, Sir Henry, 43, 48, 99–100, 107, 109, 140, 147

Bedford, 25

Berwick, 19, 29–30, 41, 52, 65, 84, 98, 127

Berwickshire, 31, 42–3, 87

Bohun, Sir Henry, 10, 49, 105

Bothwell, 48, 52, 127

Bower, Walter, 12–14, 58–9

Brechin, 25

Bruce, Alexander, 39

Bruce, Neil, 39

Bruce, Sir Edward, Earl of Carrick, 20, 44, 53, 81, 104, 107, 112, 116, 120, 127

Bruce, Sir Robert, Lord of Annandale, 25, 27

Bruce, Thomas, 39

Cambuskenneth, 10, 110–12

Carse, 104

Centenars, 89

Clackmannanshire, 41

Clifford, Sir Robert, 47, 54, 81, 99–100, 107, 109–110

Comyn, Sir John, Lord of Badenoch, 24, 32, 38, 48, 50, 137

Comyn family, 36, 38, 50, 54, 87

Cressingham, Hugh, 31

Crossbowmen, 61

D'Argentan, Giles, 49, 124

De Burgh, Elizabeth, 12, 38–9, 146

Destrier, 121–2

Douglas, Sir James, 44, 54, 81, 115, 126–7, 139–40, 147

Dumfries, 36, 42–3, 50

Dunbar, 29, 55, 102, 127, 132

Dundee, 41, 52

Dunfermline, 12, 146

Dupplin Muir, battle of, 48, 55, 74

Edinburgh, 20, 44–5, 54, 86, 98

Edward I, King of England, 8–9, 19, 22, 26, 28, 30, 36, 43, 46–8, 54, 77, 88, 116, 130

Edward II, King of England, 18, 20, 24, 40–4, 46–7, 49, 52, 54, 61, 67, 74, 81, 86–90, 96–8, 100–9, 112–18, 120, 133–9, 141–2

Edward III, King of England, 55, 74, 141–4, 147

Entry, the, 10, 105–6

Erik II, King of Norway, 25

Falkirk, battle of, 8, 19, 22, 32, 43, 48, 74, 77, 122

Falkirk, 98–9

Fife, 41

Forth, river, 31, 44, 99, 102, 110, 125–30

France, 23–4, 28–9, 32–3, 35, 40, 47, 84, 90–1, 136–7, 141

Gardiner, S.R., 9, 18, 75, 99

Gascony, 84, 141

Gordon, Sir Adam, 42

Grey, Sir Thomas, junior, 13, 15, 110, 123

Grey, Sir Thomas, senior, 99, 110

Hobelars, 61, 65

Ireland, 23, 90, 96, 134, 139

Keith, Sir Robert, Earl Marischal, 55, 120

King's Park, 104, 126
Knight Service, 9, 15, 64–5

Lanarkshire, 54
Loch Ryan, 39
Lorne, John of, 39
Lothian, 41–3, 86–7,
    115–16

MacRuarie, Christina, 50
Mail, 9–10, 60–1, 64–8, 71,
    104
Millenars, 89–90
Moray, Sir Thomas Randolph,
    Earl of, 41–54, 77, 91–2,
    104, 109–11, 120,
    139–40, 143
Moubray, Sir Philip, 44, 53,
    107, 125, 128
Murray, Sir Andrew, 31, 40

New Park, 10, 49, 93, 99,
    104, 106–7, 129
Northumberland, 40–1, 52,
    114, 134
Norway, 19, 25, 139

Og, Angus, 12, 50, 55, 145
Oman, C.W.C., 8, 18, 75,
    99
Orkney, 39

Paris, 54

Peels, 36, 43, 113, 134
Pelstream burn, 78, 103,
    117, 120, 123–5
Perth, 20, 41, 50
Protections, 57

Restauro, 66
Robert II, King of Scotland,
    54
Ross, Sir Hugh, Earl of, 50
Roxburgh, 44, 52, 86
Roxburghshire, 87

Scalacronica, 11, 13–15, 99,
    123, 125
Seton, Sir Alexander,
    115–17
Shetland, 39
Small Folk, 57–8, 124
Squire, 57
St Andrews, 20, 50, 54
St Ninian's, 54, 91, 107
Sterlings, 9, 51
Stirling Bridge, battle of, 19
Stirling, 17, 20, 31, 33,
    43–5, 52–3, 77, 98–101,
    105–10, 113–15, 123,
    125–6, 128–9, 132
Strathord, 19, 33–4, 50, 55

Turnberry, 39

Ulster, 39

Valence, Sir Aymer, Earl of
    Pembroke, 38, 47, 50,
    81, 127
Vintenars, 89–90

Wales, 8, 23, 27, 134
Wark, 84, 98
Weardale campaign, 55,
    143

Western Isles, 39
Wallace, Sir William, 19,
    31–35, 38, 41, 43, 77
William the Lion, King of
    Scotland, 21

Yolande de Dreux, Queen of
    Scotland, 25

EXPLORE HISTORY'S MAJOR CONFLICTS WITH
BATTLE STORY